STUDIES IN ECONOMICS AND BUSINESS

The UK Economy in a Global Context

Colin G. Bamford
University of Huddersfield

and

Susan Grant
West Oxfordshire College

Series Editor
Susan Grant
West Oxfordshire College

Heinemann Educational Publishers
Halley Court, Jordan Hill, Oxford OX2 8EJ
a division of Reed Educational & Professional Publishing Ltd

OXFORD MELBOURNE AUCKLAND
JOHANNESBURG BLANTYRE GABORONE
IBADAN PORTSMOUTH (NH) USA CHICAGO

Heinemann is a registered trademark of Reed Educational & Professional Publishing Ltd

Text © Colin Bamford and Susan Grant, 2000

First published in 2000

04 03 02 01 00
9 8 7 6 5 4 3 2 1

British Library Cataloguing in Publication Data
A catalogue record for this book is available from the British Library

ISBN 0 435 33046 2

Typeset by Techtype
Printed and bound in Great Britain by Biddles Ltd, Guildford

Acknowledgements
The authors would like to thank Karen Brooke for help with word processing and Sally Hurley for help with reprographics.

The publishers would like to thank the following for permission to reproduce copyright material:

The AQA for the questions on pp. 44, 59, 105, 107 (AQA examination questions are reproduced by permission of the Assessment and Qualification Alliance); The Bank of England for the material on pp. 39, 60–1, York Publishing Services Ltd for use of the *British Economy Survey* material on p. 66, Datastream for graphs on pp. 2,18, 66, 84; © The Economist Newspaper Ltd, London for the data on p. 100 and the articles on pp. 10, 63, 78; London Examinations, a division of Edexcel, for the questions on pp.14–15, 30–1, 44–5, 60–1, 76, 91, 119; The *Financial Times* for articles on pp. 2, 58, 65, 75, 84, 97, 103, 105–6, 109, 118; *The Guardian* for articles on pp. 76–7, 83, 90, 112,113,120; HSBC for the material on p73; The International Monetary Fund for data on p. 57; The Independent Syndication for articles on pp. 18, 87, 110; Lloyds-TSB *Economic Bulletin* for material on p. 95; © Times Newspapers for the graph on p. 117 and for articles on pp. 22, 96, 85; The National Institute of Economic and Social Research for data on pp. 6, 8, 86, 101; The OCR for questions on pp. 91, 92, 105 (reproduced with the kind permission of the OCR); the OECD for data on pp. 21, 24, 26, 27, 29; National Statistics © Crown Copyright for material on pp. 3, 15, 44, 48; The Press Association for the article on p. 75, The Daily Telegraph for articles on pp. 34, 75; The World Bank for the material on p. 67.

The publishers have made every effort to contact copyright holders. However, if any material has been incorrectly acknowledged, the publishers would be pleased to correct this at the earliest opportunity.

Tel: 01865 888058 www.heinemann.co.uk

Contents

Preface

This book has been produced for, and to be entirely compatible with, the new 'Curriculum 2000' AS A level specifications in Economics. It is particularly appropriate for the teaching of:

- OCR's Module 2883 – The National and International Economy, and Module 2887 – The UK Economy
- Edexcel's Unit 3 – Managing the Economy, and Unit 6 – The UK in the Global Economy
- AQA's Module 2 – The National Economy, and Module 6 – Government Policy, the National and International Economy.

The book should also be helpful for students of Economics degree level, HND and international examination courses.

Professor Colin Bamford is Head of Transport and Logistics at the University of Huddersfield and is a Chief Examiner in Economics with a major awarding body. He has written a number of economics books, including the justifiably popular *Transport Economics* published by Heinemann Educational.

Susan Grant is a Lecturer in Economics at West Oxfordshire College and a Principal Examiner. She is the author of a number of economics books and a regular contributor to the British Economy Survey.

Susan Grant
Series Editor

Introduction

This book examines the performance of the UK economy and how the UK government influences that performance. As its title indicates, it also takes a wider perspective by comparing the performance of the UK economy with that of other major countries and the 'euro area' as a whole and by examining the influence of their policies and those of international organizations on the UK.

In Chapter 1, the concepts of aggregate demand and aggregate supply are discussed and related to recent events in the UK and other major economies. Chapter 2 examines the recent performance of the UK economy in terms of four key indicators: unemployment, inflation, the balance of payments and economic growth. It compares the UK's economic performance with that of four other leading economies (France, Germany, Japan, the US) and the euro area.

To improve economic performance, governments make use of a range of policy instruments. These are examined in Chapter 3 which discusses government policy in the light of recent developments in the use of policy instruments and related government objectives.

The performance of the UK economy and the operation of UK economic policy is heavily influenced by the world economy. Chapter 4 focuses on the international economy. The sections of the balance of payments are explained, and the UK's recent balance of payments performance and pattern of international trade are explored. The principles behind international trade are also examined.

Chapter 5 concentrates on the impact that globalization is having on the UK and, of course, on the world economy. It explains the main features, causes and consequences of globalization and discusses the arguments for and against the UK joining EMU (Economic and Monetary Union).

In Chapter 6, inflation and unemployment are explored. Their causes and consequences and the relationship between the two are discussed, and the possibility that we are entering a new period of low inflation and low unemployment is examined. This idea that economic performance is changing for the better is picked up again in Chapter 7, which discusses economic growth including the causes and consequences of economic growth, and business cycles.

Finally, Chapter 8 examines the implications of globalization for the operation of UK government economic policy and for the role of national and international organizations.

Chapter One

Operation of the national economy

'No area of economics is today more vital to a nation's success than its macroeconomic performance.'
Paul Samuelson and William Nordhaus

Economic activity

The term '**economic activity**' is one that is widely used in a general way to describe what is produced in an economy. Consequently, if the level of output and the employment level in the economy are high then it is usual to conclude that the economy is doing well. From a more technical standpoint it might be said that the economy's performance is good if it has a high and sustainable level of economic activity.

Economic activity, though, can also create its own problems, as we shall see in Chapters 6 and 7. If total demand is not matched by the

Fresh evidence of strong domestic demand has added to pressure for further rises in interest rates

Official figures published yesterday revealed startling upward revisions to all the big components of domestic expenditure. The revisions to demand will worry the hawkish members of the Bank of England's Monetary Policy Committee, which has warned several times in recent months that demand must moderate to prevent inflation from taking off.

Investment and general government spending grew faster than thought in the final three months of 1999, said the Office for National Statistics.

Government expenditure was

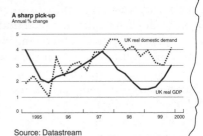

A sharp pick-up
Annual % change

UK real domestic demand

UK real GDP

1995   96   97   98   99   2000

Source: Datastream

growing at its fastest rate in 25 years – rising 4.4 per cent in the fourth quarter from a year ago. Overall growth in domestic demand continued to outpace economic output.

Financial Times, 28 March 2000

growth in what the country can produce, then there will be problems of inflation and for the balance of payments. Conversely if economic activity is sluggish, unemployment will occur.

Some of these concerns for the recent well-being of the UK economy are shown in the extract 'Domestic demand adds pressure for interest rate rises'. In order to appreciate the issues involved, it is necessary to understand what is meant by two key economic variables, 'aggregate demand' and 'aggregate supply', and how they can explain the main problems in the modern macro-economy.

Aggregate demand

Economists call total spending on domestic output **aggregate demand (AD)**. The article from the *Financial Times* referred to two of the components of aggregate demand. In total there are four:

- *consumer spending* (C): household spending on items such as clothes, food, and entertainment
- **investment** (I): spending by firms on capital goods including machinery, buildings and delivery vehicles
- **government spending** (G): spending by central and local government on items such as education, health and defence
- **net exports** (X – M): spending by foreigners on the country's products (exports, X) minus domestic spending on foreign countries' products (imports, M).

So aggregate demand is **consumption**, investment, government spending and net exports. It is often expressed as AD = C + I + G + (X – M).

In the UK, as Table 1 shows, consumption is the largest component of aggregate demand, and one which has been growing in relative

Table 1 Composition of UK aggregate demand (percentages)

	Consumption	Investment	Government spending	Net exports	Exports	Imports
1995	63.7	16.9	19.7	–0.4	28.4	28.8
1996	64.4	16.9	19.5	–0.9	29.7	30.6
1997	64.6	17.8	18.6	–1.1	31.2	32.3
1998	65.3	19.4	18.3	–3.2	31.3	34.5
1999	66.7	19.3	18.8	–4.7	31.6	36.3

Source: based on Table 1.2, *Monthly Digest of Statistics*, ONS, April 2000

importance in recent years. In most industrial economies consumption is around 60 per cent of aggregate demand, but it is significantly higher in poorer countries such as Ethiopia, Mali and Bangladesh.

In all the years shown in the table, net trade made a negative contribution to aggregate demand. The figures for exports and imports show that international trade is significant for the UK. A third of what we buy comes from abroad, and nearly a third of what we make is bought by people abroad. Some others countries are less open to international trade. For example, the USA imports less than 10 per cent of the products it consumes and exports less than 10 per cent of what it produces. However, as the USA economy consumes and produces more than any other country, the values of its exports and imports dwarf those of the UK.

Investment is a relatively volatile component of the UK's aggregate demand and as a percentage is lower than that of a number of our competitors, including Japan and Germany.

The proportion accounted for by government spending is between 10 and 20 per cent for most European Union (EU) countries. The more services the government provides the higher this percentage becomes.

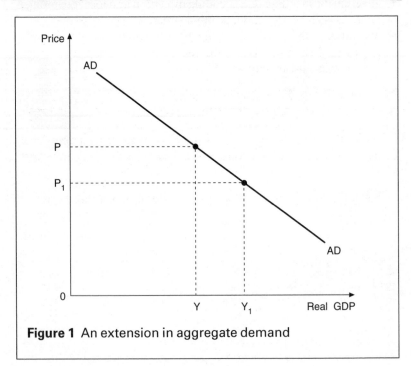

Figure 1 An extension in aggregate demand

The shape of the aggregate demand curve

Aggregate demand for any economy's products is influenced by the price level operating in that economy. The aggregate demand curve shows total planned spending at different price levels as shown in Figure 1. It slopes down from left to right as a fall in the price level will cause an extension in aggregate demand.

As a consequence, lower domestic prices:

- make the country's products more price competitive, thereby causing exports to rise and imports to fall
- reduce the rate of interest, thereby stimulating investment and consumption
- increase the value of money that people have in bank and building society accounts, encouraging people to spend more.

Shifts in aggregate demand

An *increase* in aggregate demand will shift the AD curve to the right, whereas a *decrease* in AD is illustrated by a shift to the left. Figure 2 illustrates these shifts.

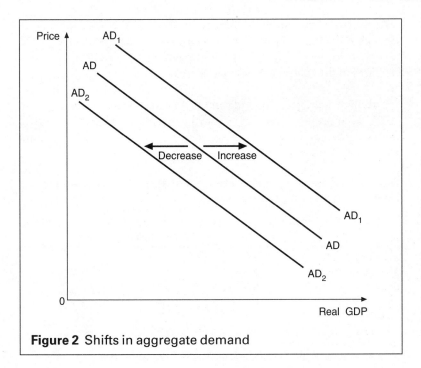

Figure 2 Shifts in aggregate demand

Table 2 Causes of increases in the components of aggregate demand

Causes of increases in consumption	Causes of increases in government spending
* increased confidence	* increase in population
* reduction in tax rates	* increase in average age of population
* increase in state benefits	* rise in crime levels
* reduction in interest rates	* increase in external threats to the country
* increase in the money supply	* rise in pollution levels
* expected inflation	* increase in the complexity and expense of
* increase in wealth	medical operations possible
Causes of increases in investment	**Causes of increases in net exports**
* increased confidence	* fall in the exchange rate
* reduction in corporation tax	* rise in income in other countries
* reduction in interest rates	* improved marketing of domestic
* advances in technology	products
* increase in investment subsidies	* rise in quality of domestic products

Aggregate demand will increase if any of the components of aggregate demand increase for reasons other than a change in the general price level. Table 2 outlines some of the possible causes of increases in the components of aggregate demand.

Although aggregate demand can fall – as for instance it did in Japan in 1998 – it usually increases. Table 3 shows how the components of aggregate demand changed in five major economies and in the euro area (the EU countries operating the single currency) in 1999.

Table 3 Changes in the components of aggregate demand in 1999 (% change on previous year)

	Consumption	Investment	Government spending	Net exports
France	2.3	7.7	1.9	0.1
Germany	2.1	2.3	0.2	−0.8
Japan	1.2	−5.8	5.3	−0.3
UK	3.9	5.0	4.4	−1.6
USA	5.2	8.3	5.7	−0.8
Euro area	2.5	5.2	1.2	−0.6

Source: *National Institute Economic Review*, no. 172, April 2000

Aggregate supply

Rises in aggregate demand are likely to stimulate a rise in the amount that firms sell. The total output that firms are willing and able to supply is called **aggregate supply**. Economists distinguish between short-run and long-run aggregate supply.

The short-run aggregate supply curve

The **short-run aggregate supply** (SRAS) curve shows the relationship between output and the price level in the period of time when the money wage rate and the price of other factors of production remain unchanged.

A rise in the price level results in an extension in aggregate supply as shown in Figure 3. The SRAS slopes upwards for the following reasons:

- Whilst wage rates and other costs are assumed not to change in the short run, to produce more may raise unit costs as overtime rates may have to be paid and less efficient factors of production employed. So to persuade firms to raise their output, the price level has to rise.
- A rise in the price level is likely to increase profit margins. This is because it usually takes some time for wages and other costs to rise in line with the rise in the price level.

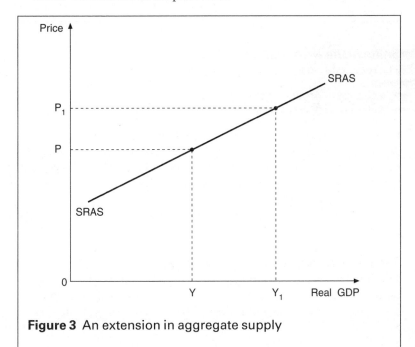

Figure 3 An extension in aggregate supply

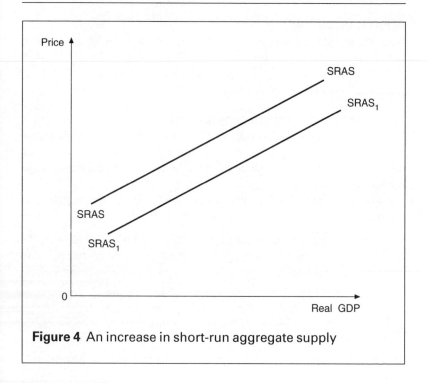

Figure 4 An increase in short-run aggregate supply

Shifts in the SRAS curve

The two main causes of a shift in the SRAS curve are:

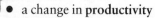

- a change in **productivity**
- a change in costs of production.

For example, a rise in labour productivity will *reduce* wage costs and encourage firms to raise their output at any given price level. This will shift the SRAS curve to the right as shown in Figure 4. An *increase* in raw material costs, in contrast, will shift the SRAS curve to the left.

Table 4 shows the changes in productivity in five countries over the last five years.

The long-run aggregate supply curve

The **long-run aggregate supply** (LRAS) curve shows the maximum output which can be produced with all resources employed with given technological knowledge. It is drawn as a straight vertical line (Figure 5).

Table 4 Percentage changes in productivity 1995–99

	1995	1996	1997	1998	1999
France	0.9	1.0	1.4	1.7	1.1
Germany	1.9	1.5	2.4	1.5	1.0
Japan	1.3	4.7	0.5	−1.9	1.1
UK	1.9	1.6	1.6	1.0	1.4
USA	1.2	2.2	1.9	2.8	2.6

Source: Table 13, *National Institute Economic Review*, no. 173, July 2000

In the short run, it is usually possible to increase output whatever the level of employment of resources. This is because, for instance, workers can work overtime. However, in the long run a supply constraint will exist. Once the economy is using all its resources it will not be able to produce any more.

To be able to produce more, the quantity and/or quality of resources has to rise. Table 5 identifies some of the possible causes of an increase in an economy's productive capacity – and hence a shift to the right of the LRAS curve.

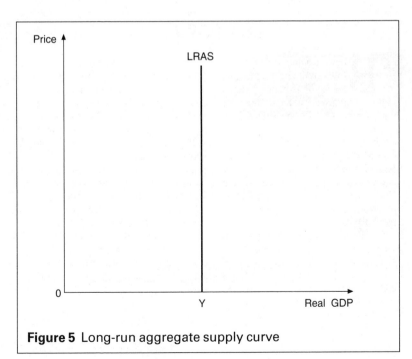

Figure 5 Long-run aggregate supply curve

Table 5 Examples of causes of an increase in long-run aggregate supply

Quantity of resources	Quality of resources
Natural increase in population	Improvements in education
Net immigration	Improvements in training
Increase in participation of women in the labour force	Advances in technology
	Advances in healthcare
Increase in net investment	Increases in those going on to HE

The extract 'Go for it' suggests that for Europe to avoid its LRAS curve shifting to the left in the future it should, like the USA, start to welcome immigration.

The Keynesian LRAS curve

Keynesians argue that markets, including labour markets, are not always self-correcting and that unemployment can exist in the long run. Their LRAS curve emphasizes this point.

Go for it

'**B**ogus, asylum seekers,' bellows William Hague, the leader of Britain's opposition Conservative Party, 'are flooding the country. And Britain should lock them all up in detention centres till they can be sorted'. 'Germany ought to educate its own 'children instead of (importing) Indians,' roars his fellow conservative, Jurgen Ruttgers, the Christian Democratic candidate for this month's crunch election in the state of North RhineWestphalia.

The European popular imagination, it seems, is gripped by panic about foreigners; that there are too many of them pouring in, that there is certainly no need for any more. In short, that Europe is 'full up'.

Contrast that view, however, with some rather different observations. Because Europeans are not having enough babies and are living so long, the European Union would need to import 1.6m migrants a year simply to keep its working-age population stable between now and 2050. With Europe's unemployment now falling and its people increasingly sniffy about the sorts of jobs they are prepared to do, or too ill-equipped to do the high-tech ones being created, the continent's workforce is in need of renewal as never before. Immigrants tend to inject into stale ageing countries fresh vitality, fresh energy and an uncommon willingness to work hard at unappealing jobs.

The Economist, 6 May 2000

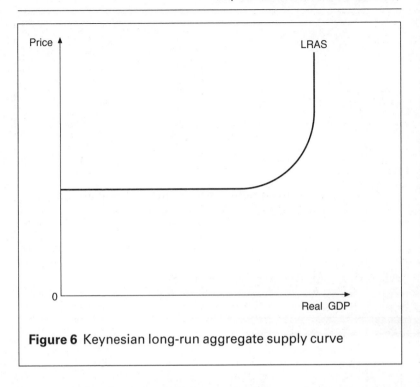

Figure 6 Keynesian long-run aggregate supply curve

As Figure 6 shows, aggregate supply is perfectly elastic at low levels of output – and hence employment. To attract more workers and to buy more capital and raw materials, firms do not have to raise the wage rates and the prices they pay for capital goods and raw materials. However, labour shortages arise as the economy approaches full employment; and so firms, in competing for increasingly scarce workers, bid up wages and the price of capital goods and raw materials. When full employment is reached it is not possible to produce any more, and the LRAS curve then becomes vertical.

Equilibrium output

The equilibrium output and price level occur where aggregate demand and supply are equal. Figure 7 shows the economy being in short-run equilibrium.

This output may not be at the long-run equilibrium output. As noted above, for example, it is possible that the economy may in the short run be producing at a level of output above the full-employment level. When this happens, the economy is said to be experiencing an **inflationary gap**. This is illustrated in Figure 8.

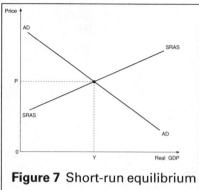

Figure 7 Short-run equilibrium

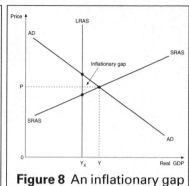

Figure 8 An inflationary gap

Of course, it is also possible for an economy to be operating at a level of output below full employment. It is then said to be experiencing a **deflationary gap**. This is shown in Figure 9.

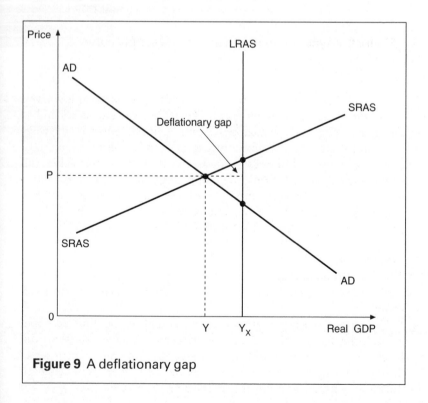

Figure 9 A deflationary gap

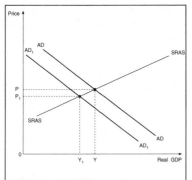

Figure 10 Effect of a decrease in aggregate demand

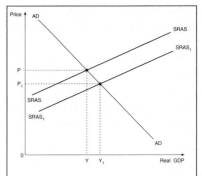

Figure 11 Effect of an increase in supply

Changes in aggregate demand and supply

Output is always changing. This is because aggregate demand and aggregate supply conditions are regularly changing. Shifts in AD curves can be referred to as **demand-side shocks** and shifts in SRAS curves as **supply-side shocks**.

In 1998, Japan experienced a demand-side shock. Problems in Thailand, South Korea and other East Asian countries – and the resulting difficulties experienced by Japanese banks and businesses – resulted in a rise in unemployment and a fall in business confidence. The result was that aggregate demand decreased. As Figure 10 shows, this caused output to decrease and the price level to fall.

In contrast, the USA is currently experiencing a positive supply-side shock. This is put down to advances in technology which are increasing productivity and reducing the costs of production. Figure 11 shows the effect this is having on SRAS and the resulting rise in output and downward pressure on the price level.

The multiplier

Increases in aggregate demand have a greater effect on output than may first be imagined. For example, in the year 2000, aggregate demand is rising in Germany as net exports are increasing at three times the rate of 1999 (in part due to the low value of the euro). At the same time domestic consumption and investment are rising because of increased business confidence. This higher level of spending will have a knock-on effect. Those who receive higher incomes from the increased sale of exports, consumer and capital goods will in turn spend some of their extra income, and so aggregate demand will rise further. This relationship between the initial rise in spending and the final rise in spending is referred to as the **multiplier** effect.

It has been estimated that the value of the UK's multiplier is relatively low at approximately 1.33 (see *The UK Economy*, edited by M. Artis, Oxford University Press, 1996). This means that an initial increase in spending of £100 million will result in an eventual rise in expenditure and output of just £133.33 million.

KEY WORDS

Economic activity	Short-run aggregate supply
Aggregate demand	Productivity
Consumer spending	Long-run aggregate supply
Investment	Inflationary gap
Government spending	Deflationary gap
Net exports	Demand-side shocks
Consumption	Supply-side shocks
Aggregate supply	Multiplier

Further reading

Grant, S., Chapters 27–29 in *Stanlake's Introductory Economics*, 7th edn, Longman, 2000.

Grant, S., and Vidler, C., Part 1, Unit 21, in *Economics in Context*, Heinemann Educational, 2000.

Lipsey, R., and Chrystal, K., Chapters 23 and 24 in *Principles of Economics*, 9th edn, Oxford University Press, 1999.

Smith, D., Chapter 1 in *UK Current Economic Policy*, 2nd edn, Heinemann Educational, 1999.

Useful websites

Biz/ed: www.bized.ac.uk/
Virtual economy: www.bized.ac.uk/virtual/economy/

Essay topics

1. (a) Explain what is meant by the term 'aggregate demand' and identify its main components. [5 marks]
   (b) Analyse the effect of each of the following on aggregate demand:
   (i) a decrease in the standard rate of income tax from 24 per cent to 22 per cent;

(ii) imports rising at a faster rate than exports. [10 marks]

(c) Using aggregate demand and supply analysis, explain and assess the possible economic effects of foreign direct inward investment by the firm LG in a new factory in the UK, on real output and employment. [15 marks]

[Edexcel specimen paper, 2000]

2. (a) Explain the effect of an increase in government spending on output and the price level in the short run. [10 marks]

(b) Discuss the factors which influence aggregate demand and supply. [15 marks]

Data response question

This task is based on part of the AQA exam board's specimen paper for 2000. Study Table A and the extract, which is adapted from *Economics Today* of January 1999. Then answer all the questions that follow.

Table A Selected economic indicators

Year	Real consumption expenditure (£bn)	Rate of interest (%)	Real GDP (%)	Employment (millions)
1989	413	15.2	654	26.2
1990	417	14.0	658	26.4
1991	407	11.0	649	25.9
1992	407	7.3	649	25.3
1993	420	5.3	664	24.9
1994	429	6.6	693	25.1
1995	438	6.5	713	25.4
1996	454	6.4	731	25.6
1997	471	7.6	756	26.1

Source: *The United Kingdom National Accounts* and *Economic Trends Annual Supplement,* 1998 editions

Consumption expenditure is the sum of all goods and services produced and sold each year. It represents around 65 per cent of the gross domestic product (GDP) or the annual output of the economy. It is the largest component of aggregate demand, and changes in consumption can have a major impact on output and national income. It follows from this that consumers' decisions can have a significant impact on employment.

Consumer expenditure is strongly influenced by households' disposable income, but is also affected by a variety of other factors including consumer confidence, household wealth and taxation. Changes in interest rates introduced by the Monetary Policy Committee of the Bank of England are also likely to have an impact on consumer spending.

1. Describe the changes in real consumption expenditure which took place between 1989 and 1997, as shown in Table A.

   [5 marks]

2. Explain how consumer expenditure is likely to be affected by changes in:

   (i) households' disposal income [5 marks]

   (ii) interest rates. [5 marks]

3. Using the data, discuss the way in which changes in consumer expenditure may have affected output and employment since 1989.

   [20 marks]

Chapter Two

The recent performance of the UK economy

'*Britain has done extremely well since 1993 by the standard criteria of economic analysis.*' The Economist, World in 2000

Views on the UK performance

The Economist's guide to the World in 2000 contains an article which, a few years ago, many economists would have thought was beyond their wildest beliefs, let alone beyond their most optimistic forecasts. Entitled 'Britain's 5 star performance', it starts by stating that 'The British economy is looking more invincible with each month that goes by.' Contrasting this with past periods of uncertainty and volatility, it provides compelling evidence that the UK has now one of the strongest economies in the EU. Look at the facts:

- The level of unemployment is second only to the USA amongst the G-7 countries.
- Inflation has been low and within 0.5 per cent of the government's target for the past two years (see the article reproduced from *The Independent*).
- The fiscal position is cast-iron and the monetary arrangements have been praised by the International Monetary Fund (IMF).
- Public finances are strong.
- Sterling has been the world's strongest currency since 1995.
- Interest rates are now lower than in the USA and Germany.
- Growth was projected to be around 3 per cent of Gross Domestic Product (GDP) for the next three years.

At about the same time, the Organization for Economic Co-operation and Development (OECD), in its *Economic Outlook*, similarly provided a very positive – albeit less striking – evaluation of the UK's economic performance:

> '[The] *slowdown in late 1998* [and] *early 1999 has been mild and short-lived ... unemployment has fallen further ... inflation has remained very subdued ... tax receipts are running ahead of forecasts.*'

Inflation at 2% slips further below target

DIANE COYLE

The government's target measure of inflation fell to 2 per cent last month, its lowest level since records started in 1975. The rate has remained below the 2.5 per cent target for 12 months, and yesterday's figures brought fresh calls from business for lower interest rates.

However, the headline inflation rate jumped from 2.3 per cent to 2.6 per cent, its highest since the end of 1998. The reason was increased mortgage costs and rises in excise duties, which are likely to take it higher still in April.

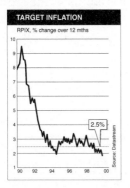

TARGET INFLATION
RPIX, % change over 12 mths
2.5%
Source: Datastream

This is the month when state pensions and most benefits are uprated based on last September's headline inflation figure. That was just 1.1 per cent, the lowest since 1963, and triggered protests over the rise in pensions of less than £1 a week.

City economists said yesterday's figures were disappointing but would not sway the interest rate debate. Most had expected the target inflation measure, which excludes mortgage costs, to drop below 2 per cent. Official figures for average earnings and unemployment, due this morning, are likely to have more influence on the Monetary Policy Committee.

John Vickers, one of its nine members and the Bank of England's chief economist, said interest rates could not be used to bring down the pound. "The exchange rate is ... a major factor in the setting of monetary policy," he said.

Mr Vickers said the strong pound had helped dampen UK inflation. "Even so, inflation had not been far below target, indicating that domestic inflationary pressures have needed to moderate," he added.

Business and unions said yesterday there was no need for a further hike in interest rates, although most City analysts expect one. Sudhir Junankar, an economist at the Confederation of British Industry, said: "We would expect competitive pressures to keep underlying inflation below target within the next 18 months."

The figures showed the main upward effect on headline inflation came from higher mortgage costs. The February rate rise was passed on to borrowers in March, while a decrease in February 1999 dropped out of the comparison.

The Independent, 19 April 2000

All in all, this is very good news – and particularly powerful grounds for the UK not moving from its current position on European Monetary Union (EMU) (see Chapter 5).

Performance indicators

The above discussion has identified certain **key performance indicators** (KPIs) for determining economic performance. These are consistent with the macroeconomic objectives of the government, namely those of:

- maintaining a low level of unemployment
- controlling inflation
- achieving equilibrium in the balance of payments
- generating real yet sustainable economic growth.

Economic theory has suggested that achieving all of these objectives simultaneously is difficult. There may be a **trade-off**, for example, between unemployment and inflation (see Chapter 6) and between balance of payments equilibrium and other objectives (see Chapter 4). Whether economic growth can be both real and sustainable must also be addressed (see Chapter 7). All in all, achieving these so-called 'demand-side objectives' presents many problems and issues for policymakers.

To get a complete picture of economic performance, other KPIs must be considered. With the increasing emphasis on supply-side policies (see Chapter 3), it is also necessary to consider:

- **international competitiveness**
- productivity changes
- technological advance and research
- education and training development.

All of these are revisited in Chapter 8.

In its assessment of the UK's economic performance, *The Economist* provides a warning in stating that 'Britain's underlying competitive structure leaves a lot to be desired'. For example, productivity growth continues to lag behind that of Germany and France, our two main EU trading rivals. Higher consumer prices ('Rip-off Britain' as it is sometimes called), a relative lack of global British companies, and the much-publicized foreign takeover of others, is clear evidence that there are inherent structural weaknesses in the British economy. Strength – in terms of traditional economic indictors as analysed in this chapter – must therefore be qualified.

Unemployment

Of the KPIs referred to above, **unemployment** is the one which tends to feature most regularly in the media. For much of the 1970s, 80s and 90s it was thought that the economies would never return to the 'full-employment' level of 2–3 per cent unemployment enjoyed in the 1950s and 60s. As a result, governments switched their objective from full employment to the vaguer concept of 'low unemployment'. However, economists and politicians are now more optimistic that **full employment** is an obtainable and sustainable objective.

Measuring unemployment

To some extent, most people know what unemployment is, particularly if they have been affected by it. In simple terms, it refers to people who are out of a job yet able and willing to work. In other words, they are actively seeking work, as distinct from those who are not only out of a job but also unable to work. From a measurement standpoint, two measures should be noted:

- *The ILO (International Labour Office) definition.* This refers to people without a job who were able to start work in the two weeks following their Labour Force Survey interview and who had either looked for work in the four weeks prior to interview or were waiting to start a job they had already obtained. This definition is the one usually applied when making international comparisons.
- *The Jobseekers Allowance claimant count.* This is a count of those people who are claiming unemployment-related benefits at Employment Service local offices and who have declared that they are unemployed and capable of and actively seeking work during the week in which their claim is made.

The **ILO method** will be the basis for statistics used in this chapter because it is an internationally standardized measure. It should be noted, however, that the **claimant count** does not include married women seeking to return to work as they are not eligible to claim benefits. Arguably, therefore, the ILO method is a better indicator and a more effective barometer of the labour market.

Recent trends in employment

Over recent times, 3 million unemployed (more than 10 per cent of the labour force) have been recorded in the mid 1980s and again, briefly, in 1993. As explained in Chapter 4, many jobs were lost in manufacturing and extractive industries. There was also a knock-on effect with service sector jobs also being lost. Since 1993, the unemployment rate has fallen steadily and consistently, reaching 6 per cent in 1999 (see Table 6).

Table 6 Selected unemployment rates (ILO), 1993–99 (percentages)

	1993	1994	1995	1996	1997	1998	1999
UK	10.3	9.6	8.6	8.2	7.1	6.1	6.0
Germany	7.8	8.3	8.1	8.8	9.8	9.3	9.0
France	11.7	12.2	11.6	12.3	12.5	11.8	11.1
USA	6.9	6.1	5.6	5.4	4.9	4.5	4.2
Japan	2.5	2.9	3.1	3.4	3.4	4.1	4.7
Euro Area	11.0	11.7	11.5	11.8	11.8	11.1	10.2

Source: OECD, *Economic Outlook*, 2000

In European terms, no other major EU country has experienced such a fall. Some smaller member states such as Sweden and Ireland (following a tremendous boom since 1997) have lower unemployment rates than the UK; others such as Italy, Spain and Greece have much higher rates. From a wider standpoint, the percentages for the USA and Japan were higher in 1999, but in the case of the latter, following a worrying upward trend.

Causes of the fall in UK unemployment

It is useful at this stage to give some possible reasons for this turnaround. These include:

- a relatively stable rate of increase of real GDP (see below), promoting the so-called 'feel good' factor and improved business confidence
- a steady flow of foreign direct investment into the economy from the USA, Japan and rest of the EU (see Chapter 5)
- an increase in the higher education participation rate – i.e. more school-leavers going on to college and university or taking up places on vocational training programmes
- a tightening of the regulations governing who can actually claim unemployment benefits.

The statistics in Table 6 and their interpretation require some clarification. For example:

- The total number of people employed in the UK must also be taken into account. This has increased very steadily over the period shown in Table 6 to reach 27.25 million in 1999 – compared with a low of 25.5 million in 1993.

- Major regional variations in unemployment rates remain. In 1999, for example, the North East had an unemployment rate of 10.1 per cent, Merseyside one of 9.6 per cent. Surprisingly, the London rate was 7.5 per cent. These geographical variations show that the UK average figure has little meaning.
- A full picture of the labour market can be obtained when participation rates, activity rates and unfilled vacancies are taken into account (see *The UK Labour Market* by Simpson and Patterson for more details).

Unemployment and government policy

As noted above, the relative success of the UK economy since 1993 has raised the question as to whether the UK is returning to a period of full employment. Some economists would see this occur when all unemployment was of a frictional nature.

The likelihood of this happening now appears more possible, but there are still the on-going structural difficulties still being experienced

Striding to full employment

David Smith

Another stunning set of labour-market figures emerged last week, with employment up to a record 27.8m and the unemployment rate, based on the claimant count, down to a mere 3.9 per cent. The lowest underlying inflation rate, 1.9 per cent, in the 25 years this measure of inflation has been collected was also announced. ...

The conventional wisdom is that unemployment at 3.9 per cent (5.8 per cent on the wider Labour Force Survey measure) is not only close to the 'full' employment rate of 2–3 per cent but is well below most estimates of Britain's 'natural' rate of unemployment – the level at which inflation starts to rise. ...

Variations in employment across the country are wide. The place with the highest (male and female) employment rate, 88.2 per cent, is not in the booming south east but in Craven in Yorkshire. The place with the lowest rate, just 51.2 per cent, is Tower Hamlets in London. If everywhere in Britain replicated Craven's employment rate, 5m more people would be in work. Areas of low employment (including more than half of London's boroughs) exist alongside places where labour markets are crushingly tight.

Source: Extracts from *The Sunday Times*, 21 May 2000

in various parts of the economy, as discussed in 'Striding to full employment'. These pockets of high unemployment remain to be tackled. However, the control of inflation in line with stated targets is likely to continue to remain the principal objective of the UK government's macroeconomic policy.

Inflation

Inflation refers to a situation in the economy where there is a general and sustained increase in prices. Over the last 20 years or so, the control of inflation has been the main priority of government economic policy in the UK, replacing that of full employment.

Its importance is reflected in the inflation targets which have been set by governments, and the extent to which excessive inflation, if unchecked, has serious implications for both unemployment and the balance of payments.

A few important points of perspective should be made:

- An increase in a small number of prices does not necessarily constitute inflation. The key thing is for the increase to be measured across a wide range of items which affect the spending of most consumers. One of the few exceptions to this is the price of fuel which, when increasing, can have a substantial effect across the economy as a whole.
- The increase in prices is inflationary if it is sustained over a period of time, not a 'one-off' rise. Experience in the UK economy over the past 40 years or so is that the general price level has increased at very variable rates in the broad range of 2–25 per cent a year.
- Under certain circumstances, mild inflation could be attractive, since it keeps businesses clearly aware of the need to improve their efficiency so as not to lose competitiveness in their markets. A key consideration is how competitive UK businesses are in relation to those in the rest of the EU.

Measuring inflation

The definition of inflation might be simple, but its measurement most certainly is not. The government regularly produces statistics on many different indicators of inflation, each of which has its uses in particular circumstances.

The most commonly used measure is the Retail Price Index (**RPI**) which records changes in the average level of prices from month to month. This index uses expenditure patterns drawn from a cross-section of households and includes around 600 items, including certain services. The weights on which the final calculation are based are revised annually.

A second much quoted measure is **RPIX**, which is the RPI excluding mortgage interest payments. This is sometimes referred to as 'underlying inflation' and is used by the government for its economic forecasts.

Another measure is the Harmonized Index of Consumer Prices (**HICP**). This measures inflation in all the EU countries. It includes most consumer products and uses more sophisticated weights than the RPI.

Recent trends in inflation

Looked at in isolation, as Table 7 shows, inflation rates in the UK since 1993 have remained low at 2.5–3.5 per cent, compared with much higher rates in the 1970s and 80s. These recent rates have been well below the OECDs own definition of high inflation (10 per cent or more), and significantly better than countries such as Turkey, Poland, Czech Republic, Hungary and so on.

According to Table 7, many of our EU rivals had rates of inflation less than those in the UK. Where UK firms were competing in European and international markets, costs in the UK will be rising in real terms at a higher rate of increase than in other competing economies. However, currently the UK has the lowest inflation rate (as measured by the HICP) in the European Union.

The relationship between inflation and employment is analysed in Chapter 6. Over the last few years it would seem that there has been a clear trade-off between higher unemployment and lower inflation. Unlike some other EU countries (notably France and Germany), this trade-off has been weighted much more towards a more balanced

Table 7 Inflation rates for selected countries, 1993–98 (percentage change from previous period)

	1993	1994	1995	1996	1997	1998
UK	1.6	2.5	3.4	2.4	3.1	3.4
Germany	4.4	2.8	1.7	1.4	1.9	0.9
France	2.1	1.7	1.8	2.0	1.2	0.8
USA	3.0	2.6	2.8	2.9	2.3	1.6
Japan	1.2	0.7	-0.1	0.1	1.7	0.6
Euro area	3.2	2.8	3.0	3.0	1.9	1.7

Source: OECD, *Economic Outlook*, 2000

approach to managing these two important variables – so much so that the UK has not experienced the relatively high levels of unemployment that they have had to contend with in order to achieve a low rate of inflation, and to meet the convergence criteria for EMU membership.

An alternative explanation, as mentioned in the last section, could be a fall in the natural rate of unemployment (or NAIRU, the Non-Accelerating Inflation Rate of Unemployment, explained fully in Chapter 6), resulting in higher labour market pressures and increasing pay claims and settlements in the UK relative to those being experienced in other economies.

The UK's experience of falling inflation in recent years has been typical of most economies. Even developing countries in Central and South America and Africa have now managed to control inflation through tight monetary and fiscal policies. Some economists have argued that high levels of inflation may well be a thing of the past in the highly competitive global market of the twenty-first century.

Balance of payments

The **balance of payments** for the UK is a record of all transactions with other economies. A detailed analysis of its structure is given in Chapter 4. From the standpoint of assessing economic performance, most attention is given to the **current account** which records trade in goods and services. Two key indicators are:

- the **trade balance**, which measures the difference in value between exports of goods and imports of goods
- the **current account** balance, which measures the difference in value between exports of goods and services and imports of goods and services.

Equilibrium in these indicators, the latter especially, could be seen as a notional objective of government economic policy.

The UK's balance of payments performance

The UK's trade balance has been consistently negative since 1982. As Figure 12 shows, in the late 1990s it was experiencing a deteriorating trend with monthly deficits of around £2.5 billion. On an annual basis this deficit was around 3 per cent of GDP. The widening gap between exports and imports in 1999 is particularly worrying.

The relative strength of the pound against the US dollar and the euro has contributed to this deteriorating position in two ways. First, it has fuelled import growth, particularly of consumer goods but also of industrial raw materials. These are now relatively cheaper and have

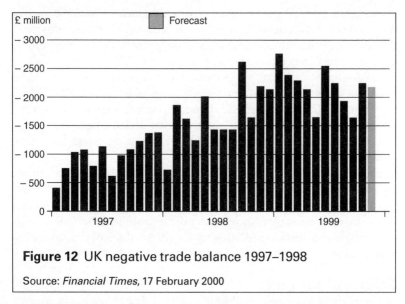

Figure 12 UK negative trade balance 1997–1998

Source: *Financial Times*, 17 February 2000

continued to replace UK production in the domestic market.

Secondly, at the same time, export markets have experienced sharp losses. The high relative value of the pound has increased prices of exported products in most overseas markets, making it increasingly difficult to sell manufactured goods – especially in the rest of the EU and the USA. Little change in this situation is expected in the immediate future, given the UK's stand on EMU (see Chapter 5) and the government's determination to keep the pound at around its current level on the international currency market.

Table 8 shows that the UK's deficit trade balance is small compared

Table 8 Trade balances for selected countries, 1993–98 (billion US dollars)

	1993	1994	1995	1996	1997	1998
UK	-20.0	-17.0	-18.5	-20.4	-19.5	-34.4
Germany	41.2	50.9	65.1	71.3	72.0	79.2
France	7.2	7.2	11.0	15.0	28.1	26.1
USA	-132.6	-166.2	-173.7	-191.3	-196.7	-246.9
Japan	139.3	144.1	131.2	83.6	101.7	122.1
Euro area	89.0	104.8	145.3	172.1	178.3	170.2

Source: OECD, *Economic Outlook*, 2000

with that of the USA – it is also less as a percentage of GDP. Within the EU, though, the UK is the 'odd one out' when compared with its main trading partners, each of whom has had a tendency to record positive trade balances over the past decade or so.

As Table 8 also shows, Japan's economy seems well on the way to recovery following the 1996/97 Asian crisis, with yet again in 1999 a very positive trade balance being achieved.

Analysis of the current balance gives a different perspective. A positive balance of **trade in services** (especially financial services, insurance, shipping and aviation) has traditionally helped to offset the deficits on 'visible' trade. Indeed, without their consistent contribution, the external finances of the UK economy would be very bleak indeed. In the late 1990s, the contribution from this source has been the highest ever recorded, making for a much lower current account deficit. This situation is therefore one which does not give undue concern to most economists.

To some extent, as Table 9 shows, the UK remains out of step on this indicator with most of its EU trading competitors. The position of Germany is arguably not as sound as that of the UK, although the OECD's forecast is that Germany will soon return to surplus on this particular measure.

The current account deficit

When a country experiences a deficit on the current balance, then it normally finances this with a surplus from its financial account, or by operating a budget surplus in its domestic economy.

For the former, short-term flows of **hot money** enter the banking system through the international currency market, attracted by relatively high interest rates for foreign investors. This means of

Table 9 Current account balances for selected countries 1993–98 (billion US dollars)

	1993	1994	1995	1996	1997	1998
UK	-15.9	-2.2	-5.9	-0.9	10.1	0.2
Germany	-8.9	-22.9	-19.0	-5.6	-1.7	-4.2
France	9.7	7.4	10.8	20.6	37.6	40.2
USA	-85.3	-121.7	-113.6	-129.3	-143.5	-220.6
Japan	131.9	130.5	110.4	65.8	94.5	120.6
Euro area	28.0	19.4	54.8	86.8	109.2	82.8

Source: OECD, *Economic Outlook*, 2000

resourcing has been particularly important for the UK economy over the last decade. It is, though, not without its problems – business leaders complain about the cost of borrowing funds, and domestic investment can be reduced as a consequence. More worrying is that it hides what are clear structural weaknesses in the economy as a whole.

Economic growth

Economic growth is measured in terms of an increase in real GDP in the economy. As such it represents an increase in real national output as shown by an outward shift of the production possibility frontier. Sustained over a period of time, economic growth produces very important benefits. The following are examples:

- *Improved living standards.* More goods and services are enjoyed by many of the population. The current generation is much better off than the previous generation owing to the benefits of economic growth as seen through a wider range of consumer goods, more vehicles, better housing and better food.
- *Increased government revenue.* Through economic growth, the government receives increased levels of taxation from expenditure on consumer goods and from taxes on incomes. These funds can than be used to finance expenditure in key areas of the economy, such as healthcare, education and social services.

Recent trends in economic growth

Historically, economic growth in the UK economy has not been sustained. Instead, it has been experienced in a series of cycles, with periods of recession being interspersed with periods of relative prosperity.

Since 1992, though, real GDP has increased on a year-to-year basis, albeit with some slowing down since 1997 (see Figure 13). Forecasts indicate that this mild slowdown will be brief, with 2.5 per cent growth in real GDP expected for both 2000 and 2001.

The reasons for this change of fortune are not easy to establish and are subject to extensive discussion and debate amongst economists. There is little doubt that in recent years the economy has had spare capacity, both in terms of workforce availability and business capacity. Harnessing this in the short term through an increase in aggregate demand will produce an increase in real GDP.

In the longer term, government policy has been to concentrate on promoting increased competitiveness through a better trained workforce, flexible labour markets, and other supply-side measures.

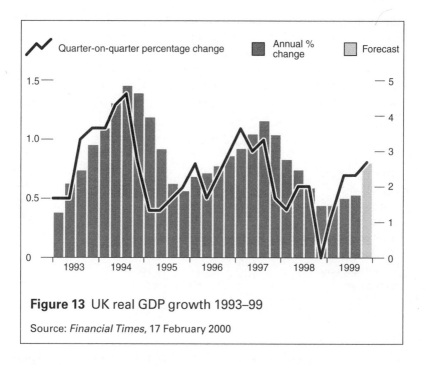

Figure 13 UK real GDP growth 1993–99

Source: *Financial Times*, 17 February 2000

(see Chapters 3 and 4). It is factors such as these which it is believed can explain why some economies grow at a faster rate than others.

Table 10 provides considerable evidence for the current optimism over the recent performance of the UK economy. In terms of growth, the UK has outstripped the other major economies since 1992,

Table 10 Growth rates for selected economies 1993–98 (percentage change in real GDP per annum)

	1993	1994	1995	1996	1997	1998
UK	2.3	4.4	2.8	2.6	3.5	2.2
Germany	-1.1	2.3	1.7	0.8	1.5	2.2
France	-1.0	1.8	1.8	1.2	2.0	3.4
USA	2.4	4.0	2.7	3.7	4.5	4.3
Japan	0.3	0.6	1.5	5.1	1.4	-2.8
Euro area	- 0.8	2.3	2.2	1.3	2.2	2.8

Source: OECD, *Economic Outlook*, 2000

although in terms of GDP *per capita*, the UK level is only about the EU average. France and Germany especially have had a much more difficult time relative to the UK. Of the other EU economies, higher growth rates have been consistently achieved by Ireland, Portugal and Spain. Ireland has recorded recent annual growth rates of 8–10 per cent, and now has an average living standard above that of the UK.

KEY WORDS

Key performance indicators	RPI
Trade-off	RPIX
International competitiveness	HICP
Unemployment	Balance of payments
Full employment	Current account
ILO method	Trade balance
Claimant count	Trade in services
Inflation	Hot money

Further reading

Grant, S., Chapters 1 and 5 in *Economic Growth and Business Cycles*, Heinemann Educational, 1999.

Russell, M., and Heathfield, D., Chapters 1 and 2 in *Inflation and UK Monetary Policy*, 3rd edn, Heinemann Educational, 1999.

Simpson, L., and Patterson, I., Chapter 1 in *The UK Labour Market*, 2nd edn, Heinemann Educational, 1998.

Smith, D., Chapter 5 in *UK Current Economic Policy*, 2nd edn, Heinemann Educational, 1999.

Useful websites

OECD: www.oecd.org/
The Economist: www.economist.com/

Essay topics

1. (a) Explain how unemployment is measured.   [10 marks]
    (b) Discuss why unemployment has fallen in recent years. [15 marks]
2. (a) What are the main objectives of macroeconomic policy?
                                                       [5 marks]
    (b) Which two objectives do you consider to be the most important for the UK government to pursue at the start of the twenty-first century? Justify your answer.   [10 marks]

(c) Assess how these objectives might conflict with other macroeconomic goals. [15 marks]
[Edexcel specimen paper, 2000]

Data response question

This task is based on part of the AQA awarding body's specimen paper for 2000. Study Table A and, using your knowledge of economics, answer all the questions that follow it.

Table A UK gross domestic product by category of expenditure (£m at constant 1990 prices)

Year	Consumer expenditure	General government final consumption	Gross domestic fixed capital information	Increase in stocks and work in progress	Exports of goods and services	Imports of goods and services	Expenditure taxes minus subsidies	Statistical discrepancy	GDP at factor cost
1989	345 406	110 139	111 470	2 704	126 836	147 615	72 712		476 228
1990	347 527	112 934	107 577	-1 800	133 165	148 285	72 232		478 886
1991	340 037	115 845	97 403	-4 631	132 252	140 598	71 395		468 913
1992	339 652	115 732	95 973	-1 699	137 693	149 903	70 992		466 456
1993	348 015	115 632	96 586	312	142 451	154 409	70 992		466 456
1994	356 914	117 550	99 417	2 917	155 566	162 731	73 913		495 720
1995	363 810	119 331	99 306	3 258	168 063	169 835	75 767	-114	508 052
1996	374 811	120 333	100 324	1 946	178 688	183 046	76 279	3237	520 014

1. Explain what is meant by each of the following:
   (a) gross domestic product [2 marks]
   (b) 'constant 1990 prices'. [2 marks]
2. (a) What does the data in Table A suggest about the state of the UK economy in the periods 1990–92 and 1993–96? [6 marks]
   (b) Suggest *two* further pieces of information that you would need to make a more complete assessment of the state of the economy in these periods. Justify your selection. [4 marks]
3. (a) Describe the changes in the current account of the balance of payments between 1989 and 1996. [4 marks]
   (b) How might these changes be explained? [6 marks]
4. (a) Calculate the proportion of GDP accounted for by gross domestic fixed capital formation in 1989 and 1996. [2 marks]
   (b) What is the economic significance of this change for living standards? [4 marks]

Chapter Three

Managing the national economy

'Economic theory is of no use to any Chancellor of the Exchequer. It is only 30 years after the theory has been developed that it actually has some relevance.' Lord Healey, former Chancellor of the Exchequer

Figure 14 shows a simplified picture of the relationship between the main policy instruments for managing the economy and the objectives of government economic policy as stated in the previous chapter. The key intermediate variables involved are aggregate demand and aggregate supply, both of which were explained in Chapter 1.

Policy instruments

The three main instruments are fiscal policy, monetary policy and supply-side policies.

- **Fiscal policy** refers to the ways in which the government is able to influence the level of aggregate demand in the economy through making changes to its income (via taxation) and to its own

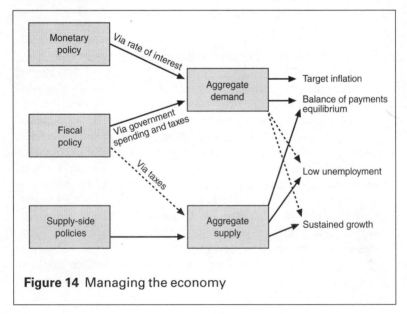

Figure 14 Managing the economy

expenditure (via current and capital spending). Variations in these policy instruments can also be used to affect aggregate supply, although the processes involved are less explicit – hence the dotted line in Figure 14.

- **Monetary policy.** Traditionally this referred to any measures taken by the government to affect changes in the supply of money or interest rates. Since May 1997, monetary policy has been set at arms length from government and is very much based on varying interest rates in relation to an inflation target given by government to the Bank of England's Monetary Policy Committee (see the article from *The Independent* on page 20).

- <u>Supply-side policies</u>. As their name indicates, these are designed to affect aggregate supply, with the <u>particular longer-term objective of encouraging</u> **sustained economic growth**. From a popular standpoint, they seek to encourage the 'feel good' factor, widely propagated by politicians. To achieve this, the policies operate on supply at a micro-level, for individuals and businesses. The government's role, therefore, is to create an environment in which individuals are properly rewarded for their efforts and entrepreneurship can flourish.

Reference to the exchange rate should perhaps also be made. Alterations to the exchange rate – the external value of the currency in relation to others – have a particular impact on exports and imports of goods and services, and hence on aggregate demand. Apart from the brief period of UK membership of the Exchange Rate Mechanism (ERM) from 1988 to 1991, the exchange rate of the pound can be viewed as an instrument of government economic policy. In terms of process it is influenced by the rate of interest, particularly from the standpoint of attracting capital inflows into the UK.

The dilemma for the government is that <u>high interest rates attract healthy capital inflows; but domestically they reduce investment,</u> <u>increase unemployment and suppress growth.</u> Lower interest rates, on the other hand, make the UK less attractive for investors from elsewhere. A <u>lower exchange rate, though, can stimulate export demand, reduce import demand, and hence increase the level of aggregate demand</u>.

The budget

Managing the national economy is a very complex task. The annual **budget** is eagerly awaited and attracts much media attention as the overall outcome is a very clear indicator of the state of the economy.

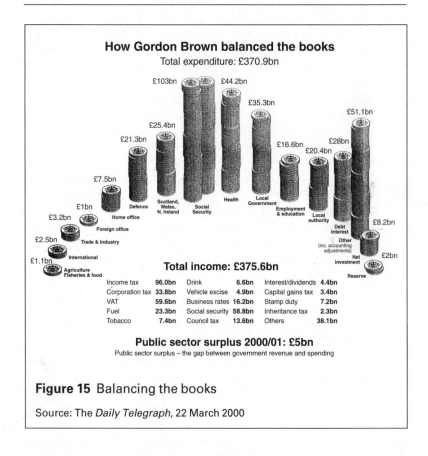

How Gordon Brown balanced the books
Total expenditure: £370.9bn

£103bn £44.2bn
£35.3bn
£51.1bn
£25.4bn
£21.3bn
£16.6bn £28bn
£20.4bn
£7.5bn

£1bn Defence Scotland, Social Health Local Government £8.2bn
£3.2bn Home office Wales, N. Ireland Security Employment & education Local authority Debt Interest
Foreign office
£2.5bn Trade & Industry Other (inc. accounting adjustments) £2bn
£1.1bn International Net investment
Agriculture Fisheries & food Reserve

Total income: £375.6bn

Income tax	96.0bn	Drink	6.6bn	Interest/dividends	4.4bn
Corporation tax	33.8bn	Vehicle excise	4.9bn	Capital gains tax	3.4bn
VAT	59.6bn	Business rates	16.2bn	Stamp duty	7.2bn
Fuel	23.3bn	Social security	58.8bn	Inheritance tax	2.3bn
Tobacco	7.4bn	Council tax	13.6bn	Others	38.1bn

Public sector surplus 2000/01: £5bn
Public sector surplus – the gap between government revenue and spending

Figure 15 Balancing the books

Source: The *Daily Telegraph*, 22 March 2000

Figure 15 and the boxed item show the details of the March 2000 budget. According to the Chancellor's plans, government spending was to rise by 7.5 per cent, the largest increase since 1992. Major beneficiaries were healthcare, education, transport, and law and order. The projected public sector surplus of £5 billion for 2000/2001 was indicative of concerns about a deterioration in the current account of the balance of payments. It is also a clear indication that interest rates were expected to rise.

Views on policy instruments

Returning to the three main policy instruments, over the recent history of the UK economy successive government's have tended to use all three simultaneously, but with differing levels of importance and influence. The last Conservative and present Labour governments have taken the view that monetary policy is the best means of controlling

---

The budget of March 2000

The main tax-related changes announced by the Chancellor of the Exchequer were:

- *Income tax* – basic rate reduced to 22 per cent; allowances and tax threshold revised.
- *Stamp duty* – increased by 0.5 per cent on the price of houses which are sold.
- *Child benefit* – modest increase.
- *Business taxes* – cut in capital gains tax; tax credits for new business research and development; Regional Innovation Fund for small businesses.
- *Indirect taxes* – 2p per litre increase in fuel duty; reductions in vehicle excise duty for heaviest lorries; increases in tax on beer, cigarettes (with hypothecation, i.e. direct funding, to NHS).
- *Pensioners* – income support threshold raised; winter fuel allowance raised.

The following main changes in government spending were announced:

- *Health* – £2 billion extra to be given over next four years; represents a real increase of 35 per cent over period 2000–2004.
- *Transport* – additional £280 million for road improvements.
- *Police* – extra £285 million for increased staffing.
- *Education* – further £1 billion for current and capital expenditure.

---

aggregate demand, avoiding the 'boom–bust' cycle experience of earlier administrations. There has also been consensus on the relevance and benefits of effective supply-side policies as a means of enhancing competitiveness and creating the conditions necessary for sustained economic growth.

The role of government, therefore, is to decide which policies will best allow it to meet its stated objectives, and to take such decisions within the much broader context of its underlying political ideology. Managing the economy therefore cannot be set apart from political reality.

Fiscal policy

Historically, fiscal policy has been the most important means of regulating aggregate demand in the economy. For much of the early post-1945 period, successive governments relied on changes in taxation and their own spending in order to attain their economic objectives.

Figure 16 shows how fiscal policies operate. This simple

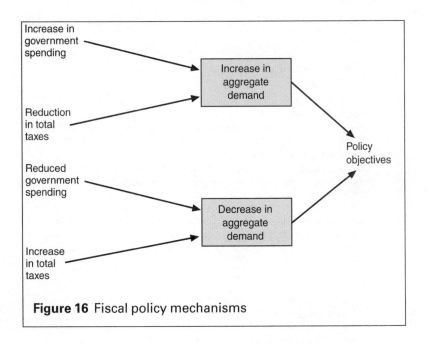

Figure 16 Fiscal policy mechanisms

representation is broadly consistent with the Keynesian approach to managing the economy. It shows how changes in government spending and taxation influence aggregate demand and, in turn, relate to explicit objectives for the economy. Consider these two examples.

Firstly, if the government is faced with a problem of rising unemployment, the fiscal response is to cut direct or indirect taxes (or both) and to increase central and local spending on goods and services or capital projects. In this way, additional spending power is injected into the circular flow of income, eventually creating more jobs. Consequently, in time, the level of unemployment is reduced.

Secondly, if the government is faced with a problem of rising inflation (this is usually accompanied with a worsening current balance) then the fiscal response is to increase total taxation and reduce government spending. This 'takes some steam' out of the economy by reducing aggregate demand, and in turn it reduces the rate of change of prices and checks a deteriorating current balance.

Assessment of fiscal policy

Fiscal policies thus operate through a relatively direct short-term impact on aggregate demand. In many respects this is their great attraction for managing the economy. Various weaknesses should also be recognized:

- Trade-offs exist between the various economic objectives. The most important one is between achieving price stability on the one hand and a low level of employment on the other hand (see Chapter 6). Using fiscal policies in the way shown in Figure 16 results in an often short-sighted approach to managing the economy; the longer-term economic growth objective; often suffers as a result (see Chapter 7).
- Governments find it necessary to put objectives into some sort of rank order in order to make clear what their priority is for managing the economy. This in itself is controversial and not always politically expedient, because it requires the government to clarify and usually quantify its objectives.
- For political reasons, governments may not always apply the most appropriate fiscal measures. A particularly good example of this is the case of the 'increase in total taxes' shown in Figure 16. All governments have problems in raising income taxes especially. This is unpopular with voters, and over the past twenty years or so it has not been used as an operational instrument of fiscal policy. There are also problems of tax evasion and avoidance, and of the disincentives associated with this type of policy instrument.
- Fiscal policies used in this way are a typically blunt instrument. They are difficult to target. In other words, all sections of the population are affected by them – or indeed all may also benefit from them.
- There are also problems of time-lags. Some fiscal measures (for example, changes to indirect taxes) can be easily applied and have an immediate impact. Direct taxes take much longer to change and their impact is less immediate. Changes to government spending are particularly slow in their effect on the economy.

The last point is a particular example of how fiscal measures can impact upon aggregate supply. Raising income taxes has a disincentive effect upon wage and salary earners. In turn, this is likely to decrease aggregate supply of certain types of labour. Raising tax thresholds on the other hand is designed to have an incentive effect, providing an opportunity for certain types of worker to work harder or to return to employment. Government spending also can affect aggregate supply. When expenditure on education or roads increases, then aggregate supply also increases. Changes in subsidies for capital projects or incentives for small firms will similarly increase aggregate supply. Fiscal policy instruments therefore can in some cases affect the aggregate supply function in the economy.

In managing the economy over the last twenty years or so, governments have consistently seen inflation control as their principal economic objective. At the same time they have been also concerned about promoting growth. It is for these reasons that monetary policies and supply-side policies have taken over from fiscal measures as the means by which such objectives can be realized.

Monetary policy

Responsibility for managing the economy through monetary policy changed in 1997 when the government set up the Bank of England Monetary Policy Committee (MPC).

Consisting of nine members and chaired by the Governor of the Bank of England, this committee meets monthly to make decisions on short-term interest rates. This important task no longer lies with the Chancellor of the Exchequer. The outcome therefore is that monetary policy in managing the economy is no longer subject to the vagaries of the political arena. Instead, it is the responsibility of an expert team who base their decisions on forecasts and inputs from a wide range of sources.

The remit of the MPC is clearly stated in the Bank of England Act 1998, and is 'to deliver price stability, as defined by the government's economic policy, including its objectives for growth and employment'. This important target has been set at a 2.5 per cent increase per annum in the RPIX (see Chapter 2). In this way, therefore, the government hopes to achieve its stated macro-policy objectives for both inflation and unemployment whilst promoting sustainable long-term growth by a range of supply-side measures (see below).

The mechanism or process by which these objectives are realized is shown in Figure 17. At first glance it seems complex, which indeed is the case. The underpinning economic logic is as follows:

- Any change in the official short-term rate of interest is followed by appropriate changes in the various market rates of interest applied by financial institutions such as banks, building societies and other lenders.
- In turn, this is likely to affect the stock market and house prices (asset prices), giving either a boost or warning to business confidence.
- There is also a likely effect on the exchange rate, such as a rise or fall in the value of the pound relative to other tradeable currencies.
- Aggregate demand, including the demand for exports and imports, will also be affected. A rise in interest rates reduces domestic

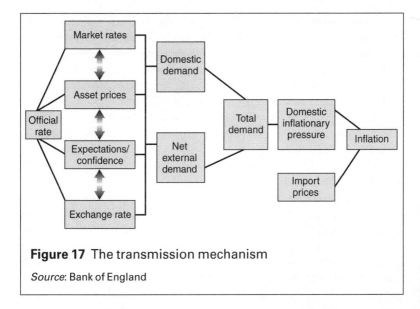

Figure 17 The transmission mechanism

Source: Bank of England

demand and demand for imported consumer goods especially – a fall will produce the opposite reaction.

● In turn, if aggregate demand is reduced then there are fewer inflationary pressures in the economy and the objective of reducing the rate of inflation is likely to be achieved.

● Finally, as Figure 17 shows, the change in the exchange rate will also directly affect import prices and in turn, impact upon the measured increase in RPIX.

Assessment of monetary policy

A particularly important point relates to the time-lags involved. The mechanisms described above take time; the initial effects are likely to happen very quickly but it could take anywhere between one and two years for any change in interest rates to be reflected in a change in RPIX.

A detailed analysis of the basis, development and main features of UK monetary policy is provided in Chapters 6–9 of Russell and Heathfield's companion text, *Inflation and UK Monetary Policy*. In summing up the effectiveness of the new policy arrangements, they make the very important point that, since 1997, inflation has been remarkably low and stable by recent standards. Controlling inflation has therefore not been the serious problem it was in, say, the late 1970s or late 1980s.

It would, though, be foolish to attribute this success to the effectiveness of monetary policy, and lately to the work of the MPC. Recession in the economies of the UK and the rest of the European Union in the early to mid-1990s, coupled with the impact of falling world commodity prices (oil excepted), have provided internal and external conditions whereby inflation control has had a much greater opportunity to be successful. As usual when dealing with macroeconomic problems, there has to be great uncertainty over the future course of events.

Supply-side policies

The growing relevance and importance of supply-side policies in managing the economy has already been recognized. The logic behind them is shown in Figure 18.

It is clear that if aggregate demand can be controlled while aggregate supply is increased, output and employment will rise and there will be a positive impact on real economic growth. Simultaneously, downward pressure will be exerted upon inflation, provided any change in aggregate supply is not overridden by a greater change in aggregate

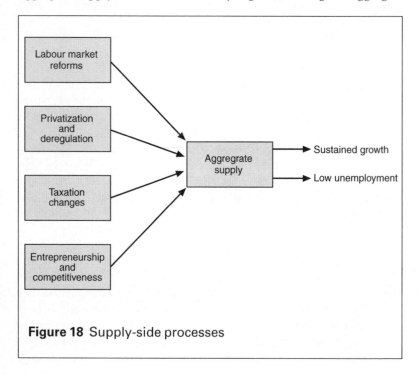

Figure 18 Supply-side processes

demand. A full account of the theories and policies can be found in Healey and Cook's companion text *Supply Side Policies*.

Going back to Figure 18, four main groups of supply-side policies can be recognized.

- *Labour market reforms*. These can be any policies that provide incentives for workers to work harder and in a more productive and effective way.
- **Privatization** *and* **deregulation** – the transfer of ownership of activities from the public to the private sector and the removal of barriers to entry. Opening up markets to competition, it is argued, leads to eficiency gains by firms and positive benefits to consumers of products of these industries.
- *Taxation changes*. Low taxes encourage risk-taking and business investment. They can also provide an incentive to individuals to rethink their attitude to work. In turn, savings may rise, so providing additional resources to fund investment.
- **Entrepreneurship** *and competitiveness*. This covers a wide range of policies, from vocational training programmes to improve skill levels, to opportunities for small firms to benefit from the changing economic environment within the UK economy. This group of policies also covers measures to improve competitiveness relative to our main trading rivals (see also Chapters 4 and 8).

Examples drawn from the first two groups will now be used to illustrate the relevance of supply-side policies.

Labour market reforms

Since 1979, the labour market in the UK has experienced tremendous structural change. These reforms were central to the Thatcher government's belief that the labour market was too inflexible and unresponsive to changes in demand. The objective, therefore, was to make the labour market more supply-responsive; in other words, to make the supply of labour more elastic to changes in real wage rates. To achieve this, labour market policy was directed to:

- reducing the power of trade unions
- tightening up on the social security system and welfare payments to those reputedly seeking work
- opposition to the EU's Social Chapter and proposals for a national minimum wage.

Such measures put the Thatcher government on a collision course with the trade union movement, as evidenced through long, acrimonious disputes with various trade unions, particularly the National Union of Mineworkers. By reducing the power of the trade unions, the government sought to shift the curve of the supply of labour to the right, thus reducing real wages whilst increasing output and employment. Controversial legislation was required in order to break down the ability of unions to take strike action and enforce 'closed shop' agreements.

Many changes were also made to the welfare benefits and social security systems as these affected the incentive to work (the 'unemployment trap', for example, is typical of the anomalies involved). The attractiveness of welfare payments relative to income from employment was reduced for various groups of workers who were thought to be 'playing the system'. The regulations for the on-going payment of benefits were also changed to provide every incentive for those who were unemployed to obtain work.

A particular change was to replace earnings-related unemployment benefit with a flat-rate payment and to put more resources into training youths who became unemployed on leaving school. Governments were also concerned about benefit fraud and the growth of the informal economy, whereby some claimants worked illegally whilst claiming unemployment benefit.

Conservative governments were also strongly opposed to a national minimum wage, which it was believed distorted the natural processes of demand and supply within the labour market. They also believed that a minimum wage would increase industrial costs, fuel wage pressures elsewhere in the economy, and be detrimental to international competitiveness.

Within days of being elected in 1997, the Labour government signed up to the Social Chapter and its minimum wage requirement. Overall, though, there is little argument that the labour market today lacks the rigidity that it did in 1979 – the outcome is that the supply of labour is much more elastic and responsive to changes in demand.

Privatization

A second fundamental area of supply-side policy since 1979 has been that of privatization, a change in ownership from public to private sector. The extent of privatization has been substantial; it has been particularly relevant in fuel and power, transport, water, steel and vehicle manufacturing (for details see *Privatization and the Public Sector* by Hurl).

Privatization is seen by many economists as strengthening the performance of the supply side of the economy relative to when activities are operated by the public sector. It is argued that under private ownership, efficiency is improved and businesses are more responsive to market needs than when they are under public control. During the 1970s especially, the then nationalized industries had a very poor public image, as well as recording poor business performances. Many of the earliest privatizations proved politically popular and were generally welcomed.

Because many privatized companies have some degree of monopoly power, it has become essential for the government to regulate their business performance through the setting up of a whole series of so-called **regulators** such as OFTEL (telecommunications), OPRAF (railways) and OFWAT (water). These regulators have been particularly concerned to get a better deal for consumers – enforced price reductions have been required following excessive profits in the case of water, gas and electricity. Competition, rather than ownership, is now seen as the way to achieving the efficiency gains promoted by supply-side supporters.

KEY WORDS

Fiscal policy	Time-lags
Monetary policy	Privatization
Supply-side policies	Deregulation
Sustained economic growth	Entrepreneurship
Budget	Regulators

Further reading

Bamford, C., Chapters 7 and 9 in *Economics for AS*, Cambridge University Press, 2000.

Healey, N., and Cook, M., *Supply Side Policies*, 4th edn, Heinemann Educational, 2000.

Hurl, B., Chapters 4 and 5 in *Privatization and the Public Sector*, 2nd edn, Heinemann Educational, 1995.

Russell, M., and Heathfield, D., Chapters 6–9 in *Inflation and UK Monetary Policy*, 3rd edn, Heinemann Educational, 1999.

Smith, D., Chapters 1–4 and 7 in *UK Current Economic Policy*, 2nd edn, Heinemann Educational, 1999.

Useful websites

Financial Times: www.ft.com/
The Treasury: www.hm-treasury.gov.uk/

Essay topics

1. (a) Explain how both fiscal and monetary policy can be used to influence the level of aggregate demand. [20 marks]
   (b) Should governments aim to influence aggregate demand, or should they concentrate on the supply side of the economy?
   [30 marks]
   [AQA specimen paper, 2000]
2. (a) Explain what is meant by supply-side policies. [10 marks]
   (b) Discuss how supply-side policies can be used to reduce unemployment. [15 marks]

Data response question

This task is based on part of the Edexel awarding body's specimen paper for 2000. Read the extract below, which is adapted from 'The conduct of monetary and fiscal policy' by T. Burns (*Economic Trends*, no. 509, March 1996), then answer all the questions that follow.

The Treasury's responsibilities include setting the framework of monetary policy, making forecasts of the economy, setting interest rates, and handling EMU matters. After discussion with ministers, we decided that the overall aim of the Treasury was 'to promote rising prosperity based on sustained economic growth'. This overall aim is then fleshed out in a two-part mission. The first part of this requires us to 'maintain a stable macroeconomic environment.' The second part of the mission to 'strengthen the long-term performance of the economy', is associated with a range of supply side policies. Macroeconomic policy has been targeted on stability, in particular low and stable inflation and stable public finances. The clear consensus around the world now is that monetary policy is the most effective way of regulating inflationary pressures and that short-term interest rates are the main instrument of monetary policy. Short-term rates seem to have a clear effect on spending, even if the effect can be delayed at times.

Fiscal policy is, by contrast, a blunter weapon. It is called upon to perform two tasks, firstly to maintain sound public finances and, secondly, to control the level of demand. It cannot effectively do both jobs at the same time. The main task of delivering low and stable inflation falls to monetary policy and in particular to the setting of short term interest rates. On the one hand this sounds rather easy and yet we know from experience that, in practice, it is intensely difficult. Essentially there are two reasons why mistakes are made: time-lags and conflicts of objectives.

One common source of conflict over the past 20 years has been the behaviour of the exchange rate. A conflict can arise because the main instrument of policy, short-term interest rates, affects many people. In particular it can be very discriminatory in its impact. It has a big impact on the housing market and may also lead to a higher exchange rate, so that exporters will be hit disproportionately hard. Meanwhile, other parts of the economy remain relatively untouched.

1. Describe the mechanism by which 'short-term (interest) rates seem to have a clear effect on spending, even if the effect can be delayed at times'. [5 marks]
2. Discuss why the author suggests that fiscal policy is a less effective method of influencing spending than monetary policy. [6 marks]
3. Explain why 'a conflict can arise because the main instrument of policy, short-term interest rates, affects many people'. [6 marks]
4. Examine the significance of the interest elasticity of demand for bank loans for the operation of monetary policy. [6 marks]
5. Evaluate the extent to which supply-side policies 'strengthen the long-term performance of the economy'. [12 marks]

Chapter Four

The international economy

'*Throughout forty years of crises and political aggravation, the EU's success story has been the substantial growth of intra-EU trade. No area of economics is today more vital to a nation's success than its macroeconomic performance.*' Lord Haskins, Chairman of Northern Foods, 1999

International trade is the lifeblood of all modern economies. The UK economy is typical, with exports and imports combined accounting for almost 60 per cent of GDP in 1998. Moreover, this percentage has been increasing over the past 40 years or so and its rate of increase has consistently outstripped that of real GDP growth. The UK's experience is typical, as the countries of the world have by and large come to depend more and more upon each other (see Chapter 5).

International trade is the buying and selling of goods across national frontiers. At a personal level, it is clearly seen through the hundreds of imported products we purchase at supermarkets, department stores and specialist shops. Similarly, the UK exports a wide range of goods to other European countries and the rest of the world; in many cases products which we also import. Vehicles are quite typical of this. British-made Rover, Ford and Nissan cars are exported to the rest of the EU whilst German- and French-made BMW, Audi, Renault and Citroen vehicles are imported in large quantities into the UK.

At an individual level, it may seem best that we 'buy British'. After all, this promotes sales of our own products and restricts the drain on foreign currency caused by imports. But if all countries followed this strategy, there would be little trade except for certain essentials that could not be produced in the home market. As we shall see later, this would also be very wasteful and the world economy would be all the poorer as a consequence.

What trade does is to permit countries to specialize in products and commodities which they can produce relatively efficiently. Receipts from such exports are used to pay for imported goods which they can only produce relatively inefficiently for themselves.

We should also recognize that our lives would be much poorer if we had less international trade. There would be fewer goods and products available for consumption, there would also be less variety, and many products which have fallen in price in real terms would not have done so.

The balance of payments

In terms of the aggregate demand function identified in Chapter 1, exports add to aggregate demand whilst imports reduce it – hence the need to take the balance of the two. Too many imports with insufficient exports will drain income out of an economy, thus reducing aggregate demand and employment. Conversely, if exports exceed imports then aggregate demand and employment are likely to rise in any one year. Over the longer term, successful trade is essentially a story of the need to *balance*.

At a national level, a comprehensive statement of these monetary flows is to be found in the balance of payments. So, for the UK, its balance of payments records transactions between the UK and the rest of the world. This record, though, is very complex, clearly more than just recording the exports and imports of goods.

New format of the UK balance of payments

In 1998, there were important changes made to the presentation of the various parts of the UK balance of payments. This now consists of:

- the **current account**
- the **capital account**
- the **financial account**.

Overall, these various accounts represent a record of the monetary transactions of UK residents and businesses with non-UK residents and businesses.

Table 11 Structure of the UK balance of payments

Current account
* Trade in goods (visibles)
* Trade in services (invisibles)
* Income account, from payments made abroad and received from abroad
* Current transfers, by central government and individuals

Financial account
Various forms of investment made overseas by UK residents and companies and inward flows of foreign direct investment (FDI)

Capital account
Transactions which result in the transfer of ownership of fixed assets such as land, or a major construction project.

Overseas direct investment and portfolio investment
Money invested by a parent company overseas and other types of investment

Net errors and omissions
A balancing item

In simple terms, these transactions are shown in the balance of payments as a set of credit and debit entries. For example, when a UK car manufacturer exports vehicles abroad this is recorded as a *credit* entry. Conversely, imported vehicles coming into the UK from elsewhere are shown as a *debit* item. How such items are paid for is also shown so that, in normal accounting terms, the balance of payments should always balance. That is the theory. In practice, an item called 'net errors and omissions' is included to cover any differences between total credits and total debits. A broad breakdown of the four main parts referred to above is shown in Table 11.

Figure 19 then provides a summary of the UK balance of payments in 1998. The current balance shows a very modest surplus, indicating that marginally more money has come into the UK than has flowed out. In some respects this is misleading for several reasons:

- There is a substantial deficit on the trade in goods – we import a lot more than we export.
- There is a substantial surplus on the trade in services, indicative especially of London's importance in world financial markets.
- Investment income, net earnings from investments, and financial assets overseas also showed a substantial surplus.
- There were substantial transfers of money from central government to the EU especially.

Current account		
Trade in goods	−20 765	
Trade in services	12 253	
Total trade in goods and services		−8 512
Compensation of employees	76	
Investment income	15 098	15 174
Current transfers		−6 526
Current balance		136
Capital account		421
Financial account		−9 025
Net errors and omissions		8 468

Figure 19 Summary of UK balance of payments in 1998 (net transactions, £ million)

Source: National Statistics, 1999

All in all it was a relatively healthy position, which would seem even better if our marginal propensity to import – the proportion of any increase in income spent on imports – were less.

Trade between the UK and the rest of the world

The pattern of trade between the UK and the rest of the world can be analysed in two main ways:

- the geographical destination of UK exports and the origin of imports into the UK
- the composition in terms of goods, services and capital flows.

A mass of data is available on both aspects. In any one year, the pattern can be described as a 'snapshot' from cross-sectional data; it is, though, often useful to look at the changing pattern over time.

Table 12 summarizes the geographical pattern of UK trade for three years: 1989 (at the onset of recession), 1993 (at the onset of the Single European Market) and 1997. Some things become clear on looking at the final columns of both parts of this table:

Table 12 UK exports and imports of goods by area, 1989–97 (£ million)

UK exports to:	1989	1993	1997
Rest of European Union	52123	66707	95949
Rest of western Europe[a]	4028	5311	7995
North America	14641	17720	23975
Other OECD countries[b]	5357	6611	10774
Oil-exporting countries	5831	6527	9788
Rest of World[c]	11605	16130	24003
Total exports	93724	119145	172908
UK imports from:	**1989**	**1993**	**1997**
Rest of European Union	70763	72022	101012
Rest of western Europe[a]	8579	9978	11341
North America	16094	18462	28065
Other OECD countries[b]	10179	11937	15192
Oil-exporting countries	2313	3801	3971
Rest of world[c]	13688	19068	29216
Total imports	121827	136177	189079

Notes: a – EFTA members plus Turkey. b – Japan, Australia, New Zealand, South Korea, Poland and Czech Rep. c – Israel, South Africa, Rest of Eastern Europe, Central and South America, Asia and SE Asia, including China and Hong Kong.

- The UK's trade is heavily orientated towards its EU partners. The greatest value of trade is with Germany, followed by France and the Netherlands.
- Trade with the USA is also substantial, accounting for around the same total value as with Germany in 1997.
- Trade with major former Commonwealth countries such as South Africa, Australia and Canada is now a very small percentage of the UK's total trade.
- There is only a small proportion of trade with less developed economies (LDCs).

Changes in the pattern of trade

Looking at this pattern over the last ten years or so, the following important changes can be identified:

- An increasing percentage of total trade is with the rest of the EU. Although still in deficit on the current account, the relative extent of this deficit is falling.
- There are substantial current account deficits in our trade with the USA, Japan and China as well as with oil-exporting countries such as Saudi Arabia.
- Overall, the current account deficit in trade with the rest of the world has narrowed in the late 1990s compared with the position in the late 1980s.

It is, however, important to appreciate that the total trade picture, not just exports and imports of goods, should be considered. In particular, the balance of trade in services and flows of foreign direct investment into the UK should also be taken into account.

Table 13 provides a summary of the current account of the balance of payments for the period 1989 to 1998. It shows very clearly a trend experienced over a much longer time period:

- There has been a persistent deficit on trade in goods with the rest of the world. In short, we have consistently imported more goods (consumer goods, food, raw materials) than we have exported, which is indicative of declining **competitiveness**.
- There has been a net trade surplus in services such as business and financial services provided by the City, travel and tourism receipts and insurance.

Recent trends in trade performance

The net trade surplus in services declined significantly during the late

Table 13 Current account balance 1989–98 (£ million)

	Trade in goods	Trade in services	Trade balance in goods and services
1989	-24 724	3 917	-20 807
1990	-18 707	4 010	-14 697
1991	-10 223	4 471	-5 752
1992	-13 050	5 674	-7 376
1993	-13 319	6 623	-6 696
1994	-11 091	6 528	-4 563
1995	-11 724	8 915	-2 809
1996	-13 086	8 897	-4 189
1997	-11 910	12 414	504
1998	-20 765	12 253	-8 512

1980s, reaching a low of just under £4 billion in 1989 and leaving a fundamental deficit on the trading section of the current account.

Many economists expressed concern about this position, arguing that receipts from privatization sales, for example, were having to fund our persistent trade deficit, and to some extent this was masking major structural weaknesses in the UK economy. Where these sales have been to foreign-owned companies (water and rail are good examples), then investment income has been generated from overseas.

The decline in the net trade surplus was also worrying. Here, it might be argued that it reflected an undermining or erosion of the UK's traditional comparative advantage in the provision of such services (see the next section). The fear was that in the global economy of the 1990s, London was losing out to other European financial centres, notably Frankfurt and Paris.

Receipts from international tourism also suffered owing to an over-valued sterling exchange rate and various non-economic factors which had a negative effect on the volume of overseas visitors to the UK.

Looking at Table 13, these economists' fears have not come about. Substantial surpluses on the trade in services have been recorded largely due to the massive income generated by City firms from banking, insurance and pensions activities. Similarly, the deficit in trade in goods has not been as great as might be expected, largely owing to the strength of sterling relative to other major currencies. Towards the end of the period shown in this table, sterling experienced sustained appreciation relative to the US dollar and major European currencies. This may be positive for the City of London, but it raises relevant fears about the competitiveness of our exports, particularly of manufactured goods, on world markets.

The principles of international trade

The economic logic which has underpinned the development of international trade has its origins over 200 years ago in the writings of classical economists who firmly advocated what we now refer to as **multilateral free trade**. Their principles of absolute and (particularly) **comparative advantage** have modern relevance in the objectives of the World Trade Organization, which exists to promote free trade amongst all countries in the world economy.

The next section summarizes the simple economic principles involved. It shows that trade will take place when countries have a clear-cut or **absolute advantage** over other countries. If we look at the UK's position, for example:

- India has a clear-cut advantage over the UK in the production of tea.
- The Windward Islands similarly can produce bananas, which the UK cannot produce.
- France has an obvious advantage in producing wine for export to the UK.

A list like this can be quite extensive; we could also compile a similar list of items for the UK's trade with the rest of the world.

What is obvious is that, under certain circumstances, trade can also be beneficial where a country may not have such clear-cut advantage. Provided it has a relative or **comparative advantage** in the production of a particular good over another country, trade can produce gains for both partners.

Summary of the principles of absolute and comparative advantage

The following assumptions are made:

- There are just two countries involved in trade.
- Each can produce just two products (say cloth and wine).
- Productivity differs between the countries, so varying quantities of each product are produced.
- Production costs and opportunity costs are constant for each product.

The production possibilities are shown in Figure 20. If each country were self-sufficient and devoted half of its resources to each product,

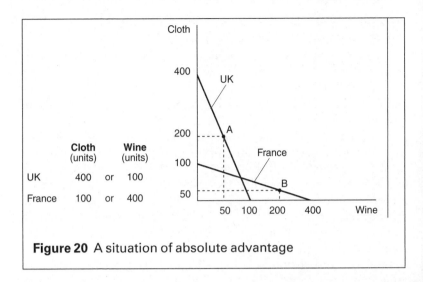

	Cloth (units)		Wine (units)
UK	400	or	100
France	100	or	400

Figure 20 A situation of absolute advantage

then the situation would be as shown at points A and B on these production possibility frontiers and in the first half of Table 14.

The UK is clearly better at cloth production, while France is better at producing wine. The UK is said to have an *absolute advantage* in cloth, France in wine. If, though, they subsequently specialized (see the second half of Table 14), concentrating on those products where they had absolute advantage, and the UK exported 200 units of cloth for 200 units of wine from France, each country would actually be better off as a result of trade taking place. The UK has gained 150 units of wine without losing any cloth, and France has gained 150 units of cloth without losing any wine.

The above situation, sometimes called *reciprocal absolute*

Table 14 The gains from specialization

	Before specialization		After specialization	
	Cloth (units)	Wine (units)	Cloth (units)	Wine (units)
UK	200	50	400	0
France	50	200	0	400
Total world production	250	250	400	400

advantage, means that one country is better at producing one product, the other is superior in the production of the other.

This rather obvious situation, however, can be developed a stage further through the principle of *comparative advantage*. This states that trade between two countries should still take place and be mutually beneficial provided the domestic opportunity costs of production differ.

Going back to our earlier example, let us assume that the UK has a clear-cut advantage over France in the production of both cloth and wine (somewhat unlikely, but remember this is no more than a simple model!). Factor endowments, including more advanced machinery, better soils and sunshine and a more productive workforce, could provide this advantage. On the face of it, there may seem little point in the two countries trading since the UK has the edge in producing both cloth and wine. This situation is shown in Figure 21.

If the UK decided not to trade at all, opting for self-sufficiency, each time it wanted more cloth (for example), it would have to divert resources from wine production. This trade-off, applying the concept of opportunity cost, can be illustrated by a movement on the production possibility frontier from X to Y. As the UK gained 100 units of cloth, it has had to sacrifice 50 units of wine production – the opportunity cost being that each unit of cloth gained resulted in a loss of half a unit of wine. A reverse movement would produce a gain of one unit of wine for every two units of cloth sacrificed. In the case of

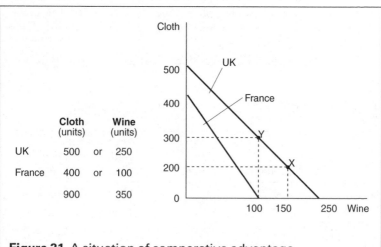

Figure 21 A situation of comparative advantage

Table 15 Benefits of specialization in a situation of comparative advantage

	Cloth (units)	Wine (units)	
UK	0	500	Total production has increased by
France	800	0	50 units
	800	500	

France, to gain an extra unit of wine, there would be an opportunity cost of four units of cloth whereas each additional unit of cloth produced would result in a loss of a quarter of a unit of wine.

The outcome of this principle is that countries should specialize in those goods in which they have the greatest relative efficiency over their trading partners as measured by the highest domestic opportunity cost ratio. So, using the data above, the UK should concentrate on producing wine, France on cloth. If this were to happen, and all resources were re-allocated in this way, total production would increase. This is shown in Table 15.

Assumptions underlying the principles of absolute and comparative advantage

The simple principles explained above are based on several assumptions:

- The exchange rate operating for international transactions must be between the respective domestic opportunity cost ratios, otherwise trade will not be mutually beneficial. Indeed, where the differences between these opportunity costs is widest, then the potential for trade is greatest.
- No transport costs are charged. In today's global economy, this is very unrealistic.
- The two-country two-product assumption is a long way from reality in the twenty-first century. Countries might specialize in narrowly defined product areas (for example, high-quality woollen cloth), not cloth in general, and there are many potential trading partners in the global economy.
- Production costs are most unlikely to be constant. As countries specialize, for example, then they are likely to benefit from economies of scale as specialization proceeds. They may also

experience diseconomies of scale if specialization goes too far.
- There are no restrictions on free trade between those countries which possess absolute and comparative advantage. This is clearly a very unrealistic assumption that has to be made.

The benefits of free trade

Notwithstanding these assumptions, there are clear gains from international trade as the principles of absolute and comparative advantage indicate. These principles are extendable, of course, to any number of countries and any number of products – the more of each, the greater the total gains from trade, as long as the principle of comparative advantage is followed.

Multilateral free trade is therefore beneficial for the overall well-being of the world economy. It ensures that goods are produced in those countries that are most efficient, minimizing the waste of scarce resources. Conversely, it is clear that restrictions on trade will reduce the gains that free trade can produce. In the interests of economic efficiency, tariff barriers and any other measures which protect the free movement of goods are to be frowned upon.

The UK's competitiveness in the international economy

Competitiveness is a term which is used to indicate the ability of UK businesses to compete in the international market for goods and services. In particular, it refers to price competitiveness of exports, and also their quality, compared with that of a country's main trading rivals. Throughout the 1990s, Conservative and Labour governments have become increasingly concerned about the extent to which there has been declining competitiveness, particularly in the manufacturing sector.

Competitiveness can be measured in various ways. Table 16 shows some of these measures in 1998. We shall look at relative export prices as well as relative unit labour costs.

- *Relative export prices and import prices*. Since 1996 especially, the former have been rising owing largely to the strength of the pound on foreign exchange markets. As might be expected, import prices are lagging behind. Imports are increasingly attractive on the home market, displacing relatively more expensive UK-produced goods. Consequently, the degree of import penetration is increasing in important industrial sectors such as motor vehicle manufacturing, chemical production, food processing and metals.

Table 16 Selected measures of the UK's competitiveness in trade in manufactures in 1998 (1990 = 100)

Relative export prices	118.3
Import price competitiveness	109.5
Relative unit labour costs	121.5
UK unit labour costs compared with	
France	+27.0%
Germany	+11.4%
USA	+11.4%
Japan	-4.6%

Source: International Monetary Fund, 1999

- *Relative unit labour costs.* This is a measure of labour costs per unit of output in the UK compared with that of our trading rivals. The measure also takes into account relative productivities. Here again, since 1996 especially, the UK has been losing out to its international competitors, particularly in the rest of the EU.

The explanation of the UK's declining competitiveness is complex, but two main reasons can be given.

Firstly, since 1996 the strong pound has made it increasingly difficult for businesses to export goods in certain markets, particularly where price competition is fierce. Textiles, clothing and vehicles are particularly good examples of such markets. Foreign customers have to spend more of their own currency to gain a given quantity of pounds sterling. British importers, in contrast, need fewer pounds to buy the foreign currency necessary for imported goods. The tendency therefore – as some of our big retailers have demonstrated – is to source from outside the UK rather than 'Buy British'.

Secondly, productivity in many areas of manufacturing remains lower than that of many of our trading rivals. Investment as a percentage of GDP is one of the lowest in the European Union; and, despite Conservative reforms, restrictive labour practices have a bearing in certain types of manufacturing. There is also increasing evidence that the UK's congested transport network increases distribution costs and reduces the efficiency of firms engaged in exporting to the rest of the EU (see 'BMW may move Rover to Hungary' on the following page).

In many respects, competitiveness is a modern way of looking at

BMW may move Rover to Hungary

RICHARD WACHMAN

BMW will decide within three months whether to shut Rover's giant Longbridge car plant in Birmingham with the loss of up to 14,000 jobs.

The fate of the factory depends on whether BMW, which bought Rover five years ago, decides to build a new medium-sized vehicle at Longbridge or at a green-field site in Hungary, according to senior industry executives.

One problem for BMW is that the company does not have any front-wheel drive platforms to develop the new vehicle. A solution could be to share platform technology with Ford, which would reduce Rover's costs but lead to the loss of another 2,000 jobs.

BMW plans to make a formal announcement about the future of Rover at the company's annual meeting in mid-May. A key factor in the German company's assessment will be how much the British government is prepared to spent in grant aid.

At the end of last year, the German group pledged to keep Longbridge open after workers agreed to swinging job cuts and Bavarian-style flexible working practices.

A review of Rover's operations will begin immediately, stewarded by new BMW chief, Joachim Milberg, who takes over from Bernd Pischestsrieder, ousted after a boardroom rumpus on Friday.

Pischestsrieder's arch-rival, Wolfgand Reitzle, also resigned after his attempt to be nominated as chairman failed to receive sufficient support from BMW's board. The bust-up was triggered by soaring losses at Rover, which is expected to report a deficit of about £350m in 1998.

Milberg is prepared to look at all BMW's overseas operations, including its pressings plant at Swindon which employs several thousand.

BMW bought Rover in 1994 from British Aerospace for £800m. But the full extent of Rover's problems soon became clear to the Munich-based group which put in a German chairman in 1996.

Remedial action has already seen the loss of more than 1,000 jobs on a voluntary basis. But the strong pound has compounded Rover's problems which are said to have been caused by poor productivity, overmanning and a weak product line-up.

Rover's UK market share has gone from bad to worse over the last year, falling to just 4.7%.

Financial Times, 7 February, 1999

some of the factors that underpin the principle of comparative advantage. In October 1997, the Department of Trade and Industry published a new *Business Competitiveness* strategy document, proposing closer cooperation between the government and the private sector to raise investment, enhance scientific research and innovation, and raise the education and training levels of the UK's workforce. In the fiercely competitive international economy, competitive edge in these areas was seen as an essential prerequisite not only for export success, but also for our overall economic well-being in the twenty-first century. The issue of competitiveness is explored further in Chapter 8.

KEY WORDS

International trade	Multilateral free trade
Current account	Comparative advantage
Capital account	Absolute advantage
Financial account	Unit labour costs
Competitiveness	

Further reading

Bamford, C., (ed.) Chapter 10 in *Economics for AS*, Cambridge University Press, 2000.

Grant, S., Chapters 47 and 50 in *Stanlake's Introductory Economics*, 7th edn, Longman, 2000.

Grant, S., and Vidler, C., Part 2, Unit 12 in *Economics in Context*, Heinemann Educational, 2000.

Sloman, J., Chapter 23 in *Economics*, 4th edn, Pearson Education, 2000.

Useful websites

The Guardian: www.newsunlimited.co.uk/
The Independent: www.independent.co.uk/
Daily Telegraph: www.telegraph.co.uk/
The Times: www.the-times.co.uk/

Essay topics

1. (a) Explain the various policies a government might use to try to reduce a deficit on the current account of the balance of payments.
[20 marks]

(b) Discuss the extent to which a deficit on the current account of the balance of payments is an indication of an unhealthy economy.
[30 marks]

[AQA specimen paper, 2000]

2. (a) Explain comparative advantage.   [10 marks]
    (b) Discuss the extent to which the principle of comparative advantage explains the pattern of international trade.   [15 marks]

Data response question

This task is based on a question set by Edexcel in June 1999. Read the piece below, which is adapted from the Bank of England's *Inflation Report* in February 1998, then answer all the questions that follow.

It is almost six years since output reached its trough in the last recession. Since then, output has risen at an average rate of three per cent a year and inflation has fallen from almost five per cent to below three per cent a year. The combination of above-trend growth and falling inflation is unsustainable and probably has already come to an end. At this stage, with output growth likely to fall sharply, monetary policy is more finely balanced than at any point since the inflation target was introduced in 1992. The central issue is whether the existing policy stance will slow the economy sufficiently quickly to prevent further upward pressure on earnings growth and retail price inflation.

Monetary policy is currently being pulled in opposite directions. On the one hand, despite the one-off effect of the higher level of sterling on commodity and other import prices, inflation has stayed persistently above the target of two per cent. Adjusting for the effects of lower import prices and changes in the terms of trade, which temporarily depress retail price inflation, domestically generated inflation is significantly above the target level. Earnings growth, especially in the private sector, has risen since November 1997 and is now at a level which is not easy to reconcile with the inflation target.

On the other hand, the delayed demand effect of the rise in the real exchange rate, accompanied by monetary and fiscal tightening, is likely to slow growth sharply over the coming year.

The scale of the slowdown depends, in part, on the behaviour of the net trade. There are two major depressing factors of this. First, the effective exchange rate is about 25 per cent higher than eighteen months ago. The impact of this appreciation on both export and import volumes is now starting to come through. Second, the crisis in Asia is likely to depress domestic demand in that region, with significant effects on world trade and output. The net trade is weakening, but the growth in domestic demand is projected to decline only gradually towards trend. Consumption will not be supported by substantial windfall gains this year and will be affected by past monetary and fiscal tightening. However, its main determinants – personal sector wealth and income from employment – have continued to rise rapidly in real terms. Broad money growth also, despite moderating slightly, still poses the risk of higher nominal demand and inflation.'

1. (a) What is meant by 'the terms of trade'? [12 marks]
   (b) Analyse the likely impact of 'the higher level of sterling' on the terms of trade and on the rate of inflation. [5 marks]
2. Explain how the factors mentioned in the passage might cause a rise in the UK's rate of inflation. [6 marks]
3. With reference to the passage, analyse *two* factors which might cause the UK's balance of payments on current account to deteriorate. [6 marks]
4. Given the information in the passage, argue the cases for and against an increase in interest rates in 1998. [6 marks]

Chapter Five

Globalization

'Globalization, in the sense of the modern form of the world economy with a high degree of freedom of movement of goods, services, capital, technology and management in response to market opportunity, is our own recent creation.' Peter Jay, BBC Economics Correspondent

We live in a world of change. Change is all around us, in our work, in our lives, and thus in the way in which the UK economy operates. The most significant change in this respect over the past 25 years or so has been the emergence of the global economy, in which the UK is just one small part. As a consequence, no single country can afford to stand alone and keep itself immune from the important developments that affect its well-being in this global context. The extract 'Rosy prospects, forgotten dangers' shows clearly how the major economies of the world are all linked to each other. What is happening in the USA especially has tremendous repercussions throughout the world economy.

Globalization is the term used to summarize these developments. More specifically it refers to the way in which markets across the world are becoming more integrated. Production, investment and trade are now organized on a global basis rather than on a national or regional basis. Globalization has two main features.

Global brands

Not only is the same brand label available in most national markets, but the product is also standardized. Perhaps the best examples of this are Coca-Cola and McDonald's. These US-owned brands can be bought not only in Baltimore and Birmingham, Alabama, but also in Belfast, Berlin, Budapest and Beijing. Prices may vary, but the product is the same wherever it is sold. Other very visible products and brands come from **multinational corporations** (MNCs) such as Nestlé, Kelloggs, IBM, Sony, Shell, British American Tobacco, Ford, Toyota, Levi Strauss & Co., Microsoft and so on. The list is almost endless and growing.

Global sourcing

This is perhaps less obvious. It refers to ways in which global companies have replaced local sourcing of their operations by sourcing on a worldwide basis, for global production. Some of the best examples

Rosy prospects, forgotten dangers

APTLY enough, 2000 looks set fair to be a wonderful year for the world economy. That, at any rate, is what the International Monetary Fund predicts in its new global economic forecasts, published this week. Amercia is still booming, and the Fund expects it to sustain for a while yet its recent miraculous performance.

Europe, with lots of ground to make up, has begun to surge as well. Best of all, for those who see diminishing poverty as the chief blessing of economic growth, the recovery in emerging economies that were battered by the financial gales of 1997 and 1998 now looks firmly established. In East Asia, especially, things are going better than almost anybody expected even six months ago. Lately it has begun to seem that the emerging-markets crash of the late 1990s – which once appeared to endanger the global economy – will soon be regarded as a mere blip in the ongoing "Asian miricle". Even Japan's grossly mis-managed economy is beginning to hobble forward.

Altogether, it is a marvellous prospect. Is it true? Maybe there is nothing plain wrong in these predictions. But at times like these, forecasts of this kind (no fault of the Fund) are especially prone to mislead. Taken at face value, they give no sense of the risks attached to the outlook. The risks this time are big and are getting bigger. And the continuing flow of good news makes it less and less likely that governments will take the steps that they otherwise might feel obliged to in order to ward off the danger. This is no doubt a pity, but it was ever thus, and it explains a faily reliable law of economics: the bigger the boom, the crueller the crunch.

Locomotive to the world

The world's economic centre of gravity, from which much of this good news flows, is, needless to say, the United States. As recently as last October, the IMF's economists predicted that America would grow by 2.6% in 2000. That would have been an impressive performance by any standards – this is the ninth year of America's current economic expansion, remember – especially when combined, as the Fund said it would be, with an unemployment rate pressed down to an extraordinary low of 4%, and an inflation rate of just 2.5%. Well, the Fund now expects America to grow by a stunning 4.4% this year, and with inflation no higher than in its earlier forecast. That revision transforms the global outlook, not just because the United States accounts by itself for about a quarter of global GDP, but also because galloping demand in America will keep exerting a strong pull on economic activity in other regions, whether it continued to be needed.

The Economist, 15 April 2000

are clothing and sportswear companies such as Nike, Adidas and Reebok, all of which produce primarily in South East Asia for distribution to the world market. Production units in their own countries have been scaled down or closed, as unit production costs in economies with lower wages are relatively cheaper than in, say, the USA or Germany. The globalization of production can also generate substantial economies of scale, helping companies to remain competitive in a testing global market.

Causes of globalization

There are many causes. Often these are specific to a particular company, but in general terms the following factors have contributed to the trends described above.

Developments in information technology

Technological change over the last 25 years has been incredible, particularly in the field of IT. The ability of businesses to communicate and handle data has developed significantly and will continue to do so. For students who are competent with e-mail, laptops and the latest version of Windows, it is quite difficult to appreciate just how much change there has been. The consequence of this is that communications are now on a global scale, and supply chains (the way in which businesses assemble, produce and sell their products) can be managed effectively at this level.

Transport developments

Real unit transport costs in the global economy have been falling, so it becomes more and more viable for businesses to source on a global rather than local basis. The bulk distribution of products in containers by sea especially has been responsible for an ever-increasing share of world trade. Specialist global logistics carriers, especially US- and European-owned, dominate the global market. Competition is now global, with companies from around the world offering their services in any market.

To be successful, these companies have to 'add value' to the supply chains of their clients. This means reducing the cost of delivering final goods, reducing the time involved in delivering them, and – with integrated IT systems – promoting a demand-driven rather than supply-led approach to their businesses. The recent merger of Exel Logistics, the UK's largest logistics operator, with the Ocean Group has created one of the world's largest specialist companies (see 'Transport combination finds that the time is right at last').

A reduction in protectionism in the world economy

Although the process has not been without its problems, the World

Transport combination finds that the time is right at last

Juliet Jowit

Consolidation within the European logistics industry has long been planned but until yesterday there had been little movement.

Only Deutsche Post, the acquisitive German post office, which has spent $5bn (£3.1bn) in the past two years, has done very much.

NFC and Ocean Group admitted yesterday that they have been thinking about a deal for four years. Their time came at last.

Now investors expect the same cocktail of globalisation, outsourcing growth and e-commerce to precipitate more action, triggered by the need to compete with the new Exel.

"They [Exel] have set the agenda and the others will have to react," said Peter Magill, head of European transport at KPMG.

Economic growth, more outsourcing and the need to deliver e-commerce purchases is fuelling logistics businesses everywhere.

Data Monitor, the market research group, forecasts growth of 3–5 per cent in mature markets such as Germany, France and the UK, rising to 10 per cent in less developed industries in Europe and North America.

Also, as customers out-source more work, they want one or two logistics providers to offer the full range of services and cover all their markets.

Exel meets all these demands: it has geographic fit – with only a few gaps in Italy, parts of Germany and Japan; it has the resources to invest in new technology and distribution systems; and it has a large customer base to generate more business.

It also has the skills mix to meet increasing demand not just for traditional functions, such as warehousing and transport, but managing inventories and optimising supply chains.

Many customers are now outsourcing their whole logistics strategy – which explains why the once unglamorous business is now often a board-level priority.

This is another where Exel's rivals will

How Exel will look

Pro-forma turnover breakdown

By region

- Asia 10%
- American Pacific 30%
- Continental Europe 21%
- UK & Ireland 39%

Global logistics revenue* ($bn)

Deutsche Post
New Exel
CNF
Kruehne
Robinson
Stinnes
Tibbett
BAX
P&O
Ryder
Hays
Fritz
TNT
Expenditors
FedEx
UPS

7 6 5 4 3 2 1 0

Data from last annual reports

have to catch up, says Mr Magill.

To trust an outsider with such a vital part of the business, customers will want to know they are buying expertise.

For this reason, industry specialisation and not just size should be the driver for the coming consolidation, he says, "Size is of course important, but so are competencies. The potential for them comes in focusing on specific industries such as automotive, electronics, pharmaceuticals, food retailing."

Financial Times, 22 February 2000

Trade Organization (WTO) has sought to reduce the overall degree of **protectionism** in the world economy. Tariffs, quotas and other protectionist measures are inconsistent with globalization. In general terms, successive rounds of negotiations of the former General Agreement on Tariffs and Trade (GATT) have helped to free up certain aspects of trade. The USA especially, of the developed economies, remains reluctant to go as far as many observers and competitors would like. As we shall see below, world trading blocs on a 'regional' scale now dominate global trade.

Reduced international capital restrictions

In order to achieve globalization in markets and products, it has been essential that exchange controls are removed or reduced and that business capital can flow freely within the global economy.

Within the EU, the UK economy has been a major beneficiary of foreign direct investment (see Figure 22). Much of this investment has come from the USA and Japan – it is particularly evidenced in activities such as electronics, vehicle production and retailing. Far Eastern companies especially have been attracted to the UK as the best location to serve the EU market. In less prosperous regions such as central Scotland, North East England and South Wales, this investment has been particularly significant, creating thousands of jobs not only in new factories but, through the multiplier process, in local suppliers and the regional economy as a whole.

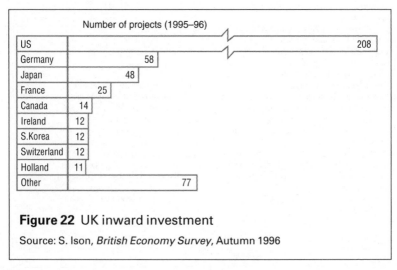

Figure 22 UK inward investment

Source: S. Ison, *British Economy Survey*, Autumn 1996

Consequences of globalization

The main consequence of globalization is that the world economy has become much more internationalized, in particular through the growth of trade and increasing dependency. Export trade as a percentage of world GDP has grown consistently to around 20 per cent in 1988. For the UK, this figure was almost 30 per cent, reflecting the growth in trade with the rest of the EU.

Table 17 shows this increasing dependency in a different way, albeit very crudely and selectively. Using a base year of 1983, it is very clear that, relatively, the so-called 'Asian Tigers' have seen tremendous growth in their exports of manufactured goods. This is particularly so for China (including Hong Kong) and Thailand. In contrast, the export growth experienced by Japan has been much less, albeit from a stronger base, but reflecting the increasing diversion of production by its major corporations to the rest of SE Asia, Europe and the USA. In the case of all countries shown in this table (except Japan), the percentage of manufactured goods exported and imported has increased over the period.

Table 17 Index of growth of global trade for selected economies 1983–98 (1983 = 100)

	Exports 1998 ($US million)		Imports 1998 ($US million)	
	Index	Manufactured goods as % total exports	Index	Manufactured goods as % total imports
Developed economies				
UK	296.7	83	316.0	81
USA	331.6	80	350.0	78
Japan	264.0	95	223.0	54
France	323.2	76	270.8	76
Germany	319.5	86	305.2	68
Developing economies				
China	836.4	85	666.6	77
Korean Republic	554.2	87	357.7	61
Hong Kong	790.9	93	752.0	87
Malaysia	521.4	76	386.6	82
Thailand	841.4	71	402.0	77

Source: *World Development Report*, 1999/2000 (adaptation)

The MNC or global company is now a business serving many national markets from a common investment base. Typically, it sources materials and components in more than one country. It is also likely to have manufacturing or assembly plants in more than one county. This is partly in response to the regional trading blocs which will be described below. Vehicle manufacturers, whose product is easier to assemble than to transport in finished form, are particularly good examples.

Other MNCs, such as clothing companies, are more likely to have factories in SE Asia and break bulk distribution centres in Europe to

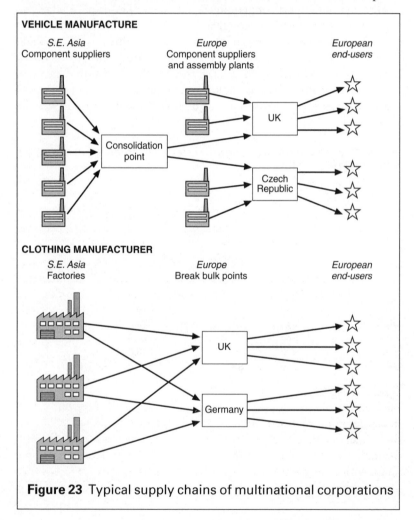

Figure 23 Typical supply chains of multinational corporations

supply their final consumers. Figure 23 is a simple representation of such supply chains. A second consequence of globalization, therefore, is that MNCs have a strong, high-profile presence in many major parts of the world.

Globalization, though, is not without its problems. In some cases, MNCs are not particularly welcomed in their host economies, in spite of the benefits they provide. A particular cause for concern is that they often source externally (by importing components from outside the country of production) and return profits generated to their base country, so causing further strain on the external finances of often debt-ridden developing economies. International hotel chains especially have been criticized on many occasions for these practices.

The Asian financial crisis of 1997/98, a good example of an **external shock**, vividly illustrated how dependent the major economies of the world were upon each other. The crisis began in Thailand when it became clear that the country's finances were in a perilous state. Its currency, the baht, lost almost half of its value in a few weeks, causing major shocks elsewhere amongst the Asian Tigers. Businesses were wiped out and the economic outlook nose-dived. South Korea followed, itself a casualty of a false boom heavily dependent upon borrowed money. The crisis was then compounded with the collapse of major Japanese banks in early 1998. Only Hong Kong and Singapore showed signs of being able to weather the crisis.

The knock-on effects on the global economy were profound. Companies based in the seriously affected economies were forced to pull out of certain countries or, at worst, to cut back on their investment plans. In the UK, for example, Fujitsu closed its factories in North East England, and Honda temporarily scrapped its expansion plans for its Swindon-based assembly plant. All of this served to show quite vividly how all the world's economies were inextricably linked. Whilst in 2000 *The Economist* sees this as 'a mere blip in the ongoing Asian miracle', the experience for the UK economy is that it must cast a shadow over our persistent enthusiasm for foreign direct investment.

Trading blocs

The benefits of multilateral free trade were analysed in Chapter 4. The structure of international trade in the twenty-first century is such that these benefits have been realized not so much on a global scale but through the increasing role of a small number of 'regional' **trading blocs,** within the global economy. Most of the world's trade now takes place within these blocs, although there is some limited exchange between their respective members.

Significantly, global trade growth over the last 30 years has outstripped global production growth through the activities of the following blocs:

- *The European Union:* 15 member states in western Europe, soon to be enlarged to include selected countries in central Europe
- *The North American Free Trade Agreement* (NAFTA): includes the USA, Canada and Mexico
- *The Free Trade Area of the Americas* (FTAA): various members in Central and South America plus Canada, USA and Mexico
- *The Asian–Pacific Economic Co-operation* (APEC): principally Australia, New Zealand, China, Hong Kong, Japan, Taiwan, South Korea, USA, Canada and Mexico.

Geographically, the most important recent change has been the participation of NAFTA members in the FTAA and APEC. The latter in particular provides a counterveiling threat to the supremacy of the EU, the world's largest trading bloc with a market of around 400 million consumers.

The process by which these trading blocs have been established are often referred to as **economic integration**. Particularly within the context of the EU, these processes have sought to merge the individual economies of member states into a single economic unit through:

- the removal of tariffs and quotas on trade between member states
- the erection of a common external tariff on trade with non-members
- the free movement of labour and business capital between member states
- the development of a range of common policies
- the removal of non-tariff barriers to trade
- the gradual merging of economic policies.

A free trade area, the loosest form of integration, involves no more than the first of these processes, often for just a selected range of commodity types. Agricultural products especially are sometimes excluded. Such integration therefore provides the opportunity for member states to gain the benefits of free trade, whilst avoiding the problems that can arise from the erection of a common external tariff.

The key economic issue is whether these regional trading blocs actually enhance global economic welfare. In theory, two main effects are recognized:

- **Trade creation** – the way in which trading blocs generate new trade and trading opportunities between members. Within their structures, less efficient producers are replaced by imports from a more efficient internal source, consistent with the principle of comparative advantage and the gains from trade.
- **Trade diversion** – this is more difficult to explain and involves the re-orientation of the trade pattern of a member state from established sources outside the trading bloc to higher-cost suppliers within it. By definition, therefore, this is not consistent with an efficient allocation of resources.

The *net* (overall) effect of trade creation and trade diversion is crucial. So, global economic welfare increases if the net effect is positive. It decreases if the net effect is that more trade is diverted than is created.

In the case of the EU member states, the UK included, the net effect is undoubtedly positive. Intra-EU trade has grown on a year-by-year basis well above that of gross domestic product, increasing not only economic welfare but the range of goods available for consumers. Trade diversion, though, is much more controversial. For the UK, former Commonwealth countries have had a decreasing share of imports – crude evidence of the effect of trade diversion. For many poor LDCs in Africa and Asia, such diversion has had a devastating effect in terms of unemployment and foreign exchange earnings. For them, this aspect of globalization has most certainly not enhanced their economic well-being.

The UK economy and Economic and Monetary Union

On 1 January 1999, eleven EU member states took the historic step of launching a single currency. The 'euro' is now the official currency in such countries, collectively known as the euro area, which account for almost 20 per cent of world trade. The UK, along with Denmark and Sweden, have opted to 'wait and see'. Greece failed to meet the convergence criteria required for membership, but joined in autumn 2000.

Economic and Monetary Union (EMU) integrates its participants by monetary means. Although it should not be confused with the Single European Market, which has sought to remove non-tariff barriers to trade, EMU undoubtedly builds upon this important achievement, by seeking to make it work more efficiently.

The road to EMU has been neither smooth nor short. Originally suggested in the late 1960s, it has taken over 30 years to become reality. Consistently, the UK has displayed considerable reluctance to participate in negotiations, let alone commit itself to membership of a group whose main features are:

- a single currency
- an independent European Central Bank
- extensive cooperation between member states on the coordination of macroeconomic policies
- a single interest rate agreed between members
- reduced business transaction costs
- a growing commitment to further economic integration.

In short, as its name clearly indicates, EMU is consistent with economic union between member states. Figure 24 on the following page shows the timetable which the original eleven member states in EMU agreed to (see *The European Union* by Brian Hill for more detailed information).

The UK and EMU

Historically, the UK's attitude towards European integration has been influenced by the worry of the trade diversion effects of EC/EU membership outstripping the benefits to be gained from further trade creation. The huge gap in the trade in goods serves only to enhance this fear (see Chapter 4). The loss of political and economic sovereignty to European institutions has also been a running issue.

These factors clearly underpinned the much more specific reasons given by the Chancellor, Gordon Brown, in October 1997, (the so-called 'five criteria', when he made it clear that the UK backed the principle of the euro but would join only if:

- there is sustainable convergence between the UK and the other economies of single-currency member states
- there is sufficient flexibility to cope with economic change
- there is no damaging effect on investment
- there is a positive effect on the UK's financial services industry
- it is good for employment.

This 'wait and see' attitude towards the single currency is consistent with the limited academic research which has been carried out. Single currencies seem to work best where economies are closely linked by trade and by the ease of factor mobility. The downside is that, where there is a major 'external shock' to the economy (for example, a significant fall in car production due to declining competitiveness), then if a country is outside a single currency it is much more able to devalue its own currency. In a single currency system, the outcome is invariably

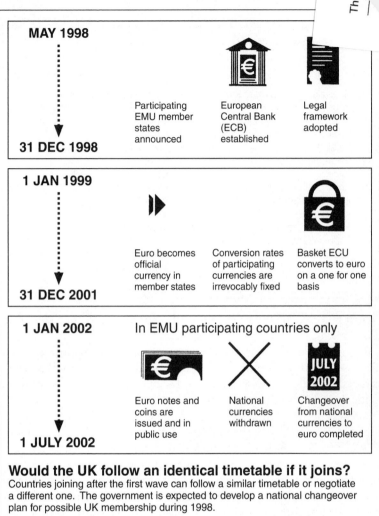

MAY 1998

31 DEC 1998

Participating EMU member states announced

European Central Bank (ECB) established

Legal framework adopted

1 JAN 1999

31 DEC 2001

Euro becomes official currency in member states

Conversion rates of participating currencies are irrevocably fixed

Basket ECU converts to euro on a one for one basis

1 JAN 2002

In EMU participating countries only

1 JULY 2002

Euro notes and coins are issued and in public use

National currencies withdrawn

Changeover from national currencies to euro completed

Would the UK follow an identical timetable if it joins?

Countries joining after the first wave can follow a similar timetable or negotiate a different one. The government is expected to develop a national changeover plan for possible UK membership during 1998.

Figure 24 The EMU timetable: sequence of events

Source: HSBC Bank, 1999

massive unemployment and a shift out of that industry into other types of activity.

The potential problem of external shocks to export demand has been a particularly important consideration, not least because in the late 1990s the general economic performance of the UK economy

The EMU debate: Should the UK join or not?

For

- Stable exchange rates are good for business confidence
- Transactions costs for businesses and individuals will be eliminated
- Permanently lower interest rates
- Lower inflation rates
- Protection against currency speculation
- Massive inward investment, especially from the USA and Japan.

Against

- Members have differing economic conditions, not the same as implied with a single currency
- The decision to join is not reversible
- Poorer members will experience higher unemployment
- Members are unable to devalue their currency
- Loss of control to a central body
- Implies a strong commitment to eventual political union.

outstripped that of the other main EU economies, as was shown in Chapter 2.

Within this framework, the arguments for and against the UK joining the EMU are summarized in the boxed item 'The EMU debate'. As this shows, there are some powerful arguments both for and against, political as well as economic.

Business in the main has pressed for the UK's full participation from the outset. So too have most trade union leaders who have feared a jobs backlash following the 'wait and see' decision. Of particular concern have been comments made by leading foreign-owned car manufacturers, who have consistently warned of the consequences if the UK does not join the euro in the near future. Some of their comments are summarized in 'Car producers' views on Britain and EMU', on the following page.

For the time being, therefore, the UK's position on EMU is unresolved. It is also unsatisfactory in so far as it has generated considerable uncertainty, speculation and excuses for what may be seen as inevitable external shock in the global economy.

Car producer's views on Britain and EMU

Toyota chief in warning on EMU
Toyota Motor, one of the biggest inward investors in the UK, warned yesterday that the company's European investment strategy might change if the UK stayed out of European Monetary Union. The warning, given by the company's President, Hiroshi Okuda, is an embarrassment to the government. He said that 'If the UK stayed outside EMU, Toyota would prefer to make any new investments in continental Europe rather than Britain!'

Financial Times, 30 January 1997

Vauxhall factories depend on EMU
General Motors, manufacturers of Vauxhall, yesterday threatened to shut its two British factories employing nearly 10,000 people unless the government signed up to the single currency. The company's chief economist said 'a lot of jobs that are tied to sale in Europe are tied to Britain joining EMU. Suppose Britain stays out and the pound, for whatever reason, remains very strong, that is going to impact on GM's decision to source product for Europe. It would make more sense for us to be within the Euro market.'

Daily Telegraph, 15 October 1997

Blair furious after BMW blames his euro dithering
Downing Street reacted angrily to what was seen as an attempt by BMW to shift the blame for the break-up of Rover on to the government and its policy of delaying a decision on the euro until after the next election. A spokesman said that 'the government has never disguised the fact that the strength of the pound has hurt some parts of manufacturing ... we will not devalue the pound artificially because that route in the past has led to economic failure and to boom and bust.'

Daily Telegraph, 18 March 2000

5000 Nissan jobs under threat as firm slashes costs
Nissan's British boss yesterday urged the government to move closer towards a European currency or risk thousands of jobs being lost in car manufacturing. John Cushnaghan, managing director of Nissan Motor Manufacturing (UK), said that the high value of sterling placed a burden on car makers which would eventually lead to plant closures. He said that 'EU monetary union has happened and will not go away. The UK has the worst of all possible worlds as we are competing outside a major currency block.'

The Press Association, 19 April 2000

> ## KEY WORDS
>
> Globalization
> Multinational corporations
>   (MNCs)
> Protectionism
> External shock
>
> Trading blocs
> Economic integration
> Trade creation
> Trade diversion
> Economic and Monetary Union

Further reading

Bamford, C., (ed.) Chapters 11 and 12 in *Economics for AS*, Cambridge University Press, 2000.

Grant, S., and Vidler, C., Part 2, Units 12 and 25 in *Economics in Context*, Heinemann Educational, 2000.

Hill, B., Chapters 6 and 7 in *The European Union*, 3rd edn, Heinemann Educational, 1998.

Smith, D., Chapter 9 in *UK Current Economic Policy*, 2nd edn, Heinemann Educational, 1999.

Useful website

Eurostat: www.europa.eu.int/en/comm/eurostat/

Essay topics

1. In September 1994, Samsung, a South Korean company, announced that it intended to build a new electronics plant in the UK.
   (a) Examine the reasons why companies like Samsung might decide to make such an investment in the UK.   [40 marks]
   (b) Evaluate the economic effects of such an investment on: (i) the UK's balance of payments, and (ii) the UK's national income.
   [60 marks]
   [Edexcel specimen paper, 2000]
2. (a) Explain what is meant by globalization.   [5 marks]
   (b) Discuss the causes and consequences of globalization.
   [20 marks]

Data response question

Read the following article, which was published as 'Record gap in Britain's trade is set to worsen' by Charlotte Denny in *The Guardian* on 24 February 1999, then answer all the questions that follow.

Britain's trade deficit with the rest of the world soared to its highest level for a decade last year as the global economic crisis ate into export markets.

Exports to the recession-hit countries of Asia crashed, while the strength of the pound priced British goods out of other markets. At home, the high value of sterling sucked in a mass of cheap imports, sending the balance on trade in goods £21 billion into the red, the biggest annual deficit since 1989.

The widening gap between exports and imports is dragging down economic activity. The Office for National Statistics (ONS) estimates that the increase in the deficit in the last three months of 1998 knocked 1.1 percentage points off growth over the quarter, with the economy growing in that period by just 0.2 per cent.

British exports to South-east Asia fell by 27 per cent last year, while exports to oil-producing countries dropped by 21 per cent. A spokesman for the ONS said this reflected the 'economic difficulties in these two regions'.

The fall in oil prices cut Britain's surplus on trade in petroleum last year to the lowest level since 1992.

Only the country's continued strength of trade in invisibles reduced the overall trade gap. The services sector posted a record £13.4 billion surplus, reducing the overall deficit to £7.2 billion – the highest since 1992.

The Trade Minister, Brian Wilson, welcomed the record surplus in services, but his Conservative opposite number, John Redwood, said the trade figures were 'dreadful' and placed the blame on the Labour government's policies.

'They have made it too dear to make things in Britain,' he said. 'They have driven sterling up too high and put up taxes too much. That's why we are not earning our living abroad as successfully as we were three years ago.'

City analysts also warned that the deterioration in the trade deficit was accelerating, a fact that could presage further interest-rate reductions.

1. Explain how (i) recession in Asian countries, and (ii) the high value of sterling have contributed to the widening trade deficit in the UK's trade in goods. [3 + 3 marks]
2. Explain how the widening trade deficit would drag down economic activity [6 marks]
3. Explain the reason for the UK's continued strength in services. [5 marks]
4. Discuss the policies available to the UK to solve the problem of a rising trade deficit. [8 marks]

Chapter Six

Inflation and unemployment

'The problem for the next two decades will not be finding the jobs but finding the people to fill them.' Hamish McRae, *The Independent*, 21 January 2000

'It is now a cliché to say the 1970s and 1980s were the high-inflation aberration, and we are now in the low inflation norm.' David Smith, *Sunday Times*, 21 January 2000

The outcome of Chapter 2 and the above quotes suggest that the UK is moving into a new era of improved economic performance, combining low levels of unemployment and inflation with sustainable economic growth. This is in marked contrast with the 1970s, 80s and early 90s which were dominated by concerns about high levels of inflation and unemployment. In these decades many politicians, economists and commentators came to believe that inflation would continue to be a real threat and that full employment had become an unachievable objective.

Now in the USA, the UK and increasingly in other EU countries, economists are beginning to reframe their analysis to fit a new economic environment. As 'A changing relationship' indicates, we may be witnessing a very significant and beneficial change.

A changing relationship

For many years economists regarded it as uncontroversial that if unemployment in America fell below 6 per cent, inflation would accelerate. Both the theory and the evidence supporting it seemed impeccable. But the facts now appear to say otherwise. It would be difficult to exaggerate how much turns on these mysterious facts, not just for America but for the rest of the world as well. If America can continue to combine unemployment of barely 4 per cent or even less, with 'price stability', then the economy has undergone a seismic change for the better in its underlying performance.

The Economist, 24 April 1999

Inflation

Causes of inflation

The high levels of inflation in the 1970s, but also in the 1980s, led to a considerable analysis of the causes of inflation by economists.

In 1973/74 and the start of the 1980s, the price level in many countries rose. The cause of this was the supply-side shock resulting from the dramatic increase in oil prices. This increased firms' costs of production, shifting the aggregate supply curve to the left and raising the price level, as shown in Figure 25. This rise in inflation spreads throughout the world. Higher prices in other countries can lead to a rise in domestic inflation through:

- higher costs of raw materials
- higher prices of imported finished products
- a reduction in pressure on domestic producers to keep costs and prices down
- increased demands for wages to rise to cover higher cost of living.

Cost-push inflation may also arise from a fall in the country's exchange rate. This lowers the price of exports, in terms of foreign currencies, but raises the price of imports in the domestic economy. The fall in the Brazilian currency, the 'real', was one of the reasons for the rise in inflation in Brazil in 1999. However, the most common cause of cost-push inflation is increases in wage rates above corresponding productivity increases. In the late 1960s unit wage costs rose throughout western Europe and the United States, pushing up inflation levels.

The other main cause of inflation is **demand-pull inflation**. This occurs when an increase in aggregate demand pushes up the price level as shown in Figure 26.

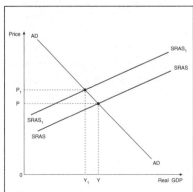

Figure 25 Cost-push inflation

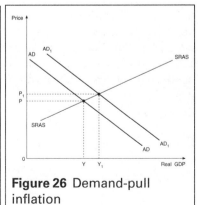

Figure 26 Demand-pull inflation

Demand-pull inflation occurred in the UK in the period 1986–89. Increases in consumer spending, encouraged by the availability and low cost of borrowing and increased business confidence arising from falling unemployment, pulled up the price level.

An increase in net exports or a rise in government spending may also trigger a period of demand-pull inflation. A number of the transitional economies of the CIS (Commonwealth of Independent States) experienced **hyperinflation** in the 1990s, in large part due to their governments financing their spending by increasing the money supply. For example, inflation soared to 10996 per cent in Armenia and 10155 per cent in Ukraine in 1993.

Monetarists argue that inflation is caused by the money supply growing faster than output. The excessive growth of money causes interest rates to fall. Lower interest rates stimulate consumption and investment and also cause the exchange rate to fall, which in turn leads to a rise in net exports.

In support of their line of argument, monetarists make use of the **Quantity Theory**. This theory is based on an interpretation of the **Fisher equation** put forward by the American economist Irving Fisher in 1911. The equation is $MV = PT$ (sometimes expressed as $MV = PY$). M is the money supply, V is the velocity of circulation (that is, the number of times money changes hands), P is the price level, and T (or Y) is output (transactions).

As it stands the Fisher equation has to be true, as both sides represent total expenditure. However, the monetarists' assumption that V and T are not affected by changes in the money supply turns the equation into the theory that changes in the money supply cause equal percentage changes in the price level.

Keynesians challenge this view, arguing that a change in the money supply can affect the velocity of circulation and output so that no direct relationship between changes in the money supply and inflation can be established. For example, if the money supply increases by 10 per cent and the velocity of circulation falls by 10 per cent, the price level will be unaffected. The box 'Views on the relationship between the money supply and inflation' on the following page contrasts monetarist and Keynesian views.

Consequences of inflation

Governments are anxious to avoid high levels of inflation because of the harmful effects it can cause. There are extra costs:

**Views on the relationship between
the money supply and inflation**

Milton Friedman said that 'inflation is always and everywhere a monetary phenomenon'. By this he meant that periods of inflation always coincide with increases in the money supply.

Keynesians and monetarists agree on this. Where they disagree is on the line of causation.

Monetarists argue that it is increases in the money supply which cause inflation, whereas Keynesians argue that it is increases in inflation which cause increases in the money supply. They believe that if inflation occurs, firms and households borrow more to finance increased costs and the government increases the money supply to ensure there is sufficient liquidity in the system.

- **menu costs**: the costs of changing prices
- **shoe leather costs**: the costs of shopping around for the lowest prices and highest rates of interest
- *increased administrative costs*: households, firms and the government have to devote resources to estimating future inflation.

Other drawbacks are:

- *A reduction in price competitiveness.* If the country's inflation rate is higher than its competitors', the products it produces will become relatively more expensive in international markets.
- *Undesirable redistribution of income.* Some may gain and some may lose real income as a result of inflation. For instance, workers with weak bargaining power and lenders whose nominal rate of interest rises by less than the inflation rate will lose. In contrast, home-owners whose property rises in value by more than inflation and workers who obtain wage rises above the rate of inflation will gain.
- *Discouragement of investment.* The uncertainty about future costs and profit levels created by inflation may discourage investment.

The significance of these drawbacks of inflation is influenced by the inflation rate and whether it has been anticipated or not. High and unanticipated inflation is serious because it becomes difficult for governments, firms and households to adjust their tax rates, prices and incomes in line with inflation. Indeed, 'hyperinflation' may destabilize the workings of the economy ,with people losing faith in the value of the currency.

Policy on inflation

The main policy instrument used in the UK, the euro area and the USA to control inflation is interest rate changes. The Federal Reserve Bank of the USA, the European Central Bank (ECB) of the euro area, and the Monetary Policy Committee (MPC) of the Bank of England will raise the rate of interest if they believe that there is a risk that inflation will rise too far beyond the targets that have been set.

The MPC has been set the task of targeting inflation, as measured by RPIX, at an annual $2^1/_2$ per cent. The ECB is obliged to maintain price stability, defined as an annual inflation rate of between zero and 2 per cent over the medium term.

To assess future movements in the price level, Central Banks examine a range of data, including current and forecasted:

- labour market data (for example, pay growth, unemployment rate, skill shortages)
- housing market data (for example, house price indices, mortgage lending)
- consumer spending including high street sales figures
- money supply growth
- economic growth rate against trend growth rate
- consumer and business confidence
- exchange rate movements
- commodity prices (for example, the price of oil)
- global economic conditions.

'UK leads way on rates' discusses how interest rates throughout industrial economies tend to move in line and how any one Central Bank's decision on interest rates is influenced by global events.

Recent inflation trends

Although inflation rose slightly in the euro area at the start of 2000, owing mainly to high oil prices and the euro's low exchange rate, inflation at the end of the twentieth and start of the twenty-first century has been notably lower in the UK, USA and EU than at any stage over the past 30 years. A number of factors are thought to be contributing to this changed situation:

- technological advances, in particular the continuing development of the internet which is raising productivity and reducing costs

UK leads way on rates

MARK ATKINSON

The Bank of England yesterday became the first of the world's top central banks to raise interest rates this year in a move which is expected to be followed soon by both the European Central Bank and the US Federal Reserve.

Against a backdrop of accelerating global economic activity and mounting inflationary pressures, the Bank of England's monetary policy committee voted to increase its benchmark lending rate by a quarter point to 5.75 per cent.

Britain's third rate rise since September is widely anticipated to be the harbinger of further increases in borrowing costs around the globe, with only struggling Japan of the big industrial economies forecast to leave policy on hold.

The Fed meets next month, with a rate rise of at least 0.25 per cent predicted, and the ECB is also expected to put up rates some time in the first three months of the year.

The Guardian, 14 January 2000

- increased global competition resulting from improved communications and the reduction in trade barriers
- changes in attitudes, with households and firms no longer expecting high inflation and so not acting in a way which creates inflation.

In the UK, two additional factors have been putting downward, pressure on inflation. One is the increased publicity, and criticism of producers and retailers who charge higher prices than in other EU countries. Vehicle retailers and supermarkets have come in for particular censure with frequent reference to 'rip-off Britain'.

The other factor is the high value of the pound which keeps the price of imported raw materials and finished products low and puts pressure on UK firms to keep their costs and prices low in order to compete at home and abroad.

The extract 'Inflation drops to its lowest level for 25 years' on the following page discusses how low the inflation rate had fallen at the start of 2000 and the contribution that the high value of the pound was playing in the reduction in the inflation rate.

Implications of the new low-inflation environment

For decades economists and politicians were emphasizing the dangers of inflation and the benefits of price stability. However, the recent experience of low inflation – and in particular **deflation** in Japan – have alerted people's attention to the disadvantages of too low an inflation rate. They include the following:

Inflation drops to its lowest level for 25 years

CHRISTOPHER ADAMS

Inflation fell to its lowest level for 25 years in March, helped by the soaring pound, official figures released yesterday show. Falling food prices, cheaper clothes and shoes, and widespread discounting on household and electronic goods have contributed to a sharp slowdown in retail price growth. The data suggests that the high pound, which makes imports cheaper and eases demand pressures, is having a bigger impact on inflation than the Bank of England expected. ...

According to the Office of National Statistics, underlying annual inflation, which excludes mortgages, dropped in March to 2 per cent, from 2.2 per cent the previous month – its lowest level since 1975 and well below the government's targeted rate of 2.5 per cent.

Annual % change in RPIX

Source: Datastream

Financial Times, 19 April 2000

- It is difficult to reduce real costs of production. The largest component of costs of production is wages. With an inflation rate above, say, three per cent it is possible to cut real wages by raising nominal wages by two per cent.
- Low rates of inflation may result in a rise in real interest rates. Consumption and investment are thereby discouraged.
- There is a risk of a downward spiral in economic activity if the price level falls. As witnessed in Japan in the late 1990s, deflation can reduce confidence. This, combined with the encouragement to households and firms to delay their purchase of consumer and capital goods in expectation of future lower prices, reduces aggregate demand. This pushes the price level down further and reduces output and employment.

Whilst the prices of services were still rising in the UK, the start of 2000 witnessed the prices of goods falling, as discussed in 'Average prices fall for the first time on record'.

Average prices fall for the first time on record

LEA PATERSON

There was fresh evidence yesterday of deflation on the high street, with the Confederation of British Industry reporting year-on-year falls in average shop prices for the first time on record.

As many as 30 per cent of retailers said prices were lower last month than in the same period in 1999, while 26 per cent said prices were up.

The CBI said the resulting balance of minus 4 per cent was the first time in the survey's 16 year history that the proportion of retailers cutting prices had exceeded the proportion putting them up. More price cuts are expected this month.

Falling prices were most widespread in areas such as household goods, shoes and clothes, for which sales volumes rose substantially.

The Times, 2 March 2000

Unemployment

The unemployment situation has also changed since the 1970s, 80s and early 90s. In those decades, unemployment in the EU and the USA reached very high levels. In the UK, for example, it rose to 3.3 million (11.2 per cent of the workforce) in 1986.

Unemployment can arise from demand-side and/or supply-side factors. A lack of aggregate demand will result in **cyclical unemployment** affecting workers throughout the economy and in other countries. Problems on the supply side – such as a lack of information, lack of appropriate skills, geographical and occupational immobility of labour, and voluntary unemployment – also cause unemployment. In the period from the start of the 1970s to the early 1990s, unemployment occurred in Europe and the USA as a result of both demand- and supply-side factors. For example, in the UK in the 1970s, rises in oil prices and increases in wage rates, driven up by trade union power, are thought to have resulted in firms laying off workers, and in the 1980s, the government's deflationary policy increased unemployment.

Costs of unemployment

The high levels of unemployment operating over the past 30 years or so imposed a number of costs, including the following.

- *A loss of potential output.* Having workers unemployed meant that economies were producing inside their production possibility curves. This meant that these economies produced fewer goods and services than they were capable of, and hence living standards were lower than possible.
- *A fall in tax revenues and a rise in government spending on unemployment benefits.* This reduced governments' ability to spend on education, and healthcare and poverty alleviation.
- *A rise in poverty.* Unemployment was, and is, a major cause of poverty in the UK.
- *A rise in health problems.* Mental health problems and a range of illnesses increased among the unemployed and their families
- **Hysteresis.** This refers to unemployment generating more unemployment. The longer workers are unemployed, the harder they find it to obtain a job. This is because their skills become rusty, making employers reluctant to recruit them, and because of this, the unemployed lose confidence. In this earlier period, not only did unemployment rise, but so did the duration of unemployment with, for example, in the mid-1980s more than 1 million workers having been unemployed for more than a year.
- *A rise in crime.* It is now widely thought that rises in the unemployment rate of young males and crime levels are linked.

Recent unemployment trends

Unemployment in the late 1990s and at the start of the new millennium fell in the UK, the rest of the EU and the USA, although not in Japan. It is thought that this downward trend will continue in Europe and the USA, as shown in Table 18.

Table 18 Standardized unemployment rates (forecasts)

	1998	1999	2000	2001	2002–06
France	11.7	11.0	10.0	9.2	8.0
Germany	9.4	9.1	8.7	8.4	7.9
Japan	4.1	4.6	4.7	4.5	4.6
UK	6.3	6.1	5.8	5.6	5.4
USA	4.5	4.2	4.0	4.1	4.2
EU	10.0	9.2	8.6	8.2	7.8
Euro area	10.9	10.0	9.4	8.9	8.7

Source: *National Institute Economic Review*, no. 172, April 2000

There are thought to be a number of reasons why unemployment has been falling in Europe. These include relatively low wage growth, the low value of the eurothe, liberalization of labour laws in some European countries, appropriate government measures and improved global activity.

Falling unemployment is infectious. For example, if unemployment rates fall in Spain, Germany and the UK, incomes in these countries will rise. This will increase the value of imports they buy from, say, the Netherlands, France and the USA, thereby creating employment opportunities in those countries.

Full employment

For the first time since the 1960s, commentators, economists and politicians are discussing the possibility of some economies, including the UK's and the USA's, returning to full employment. For the UK, this would mean an unemployment rate of two to three per cent.

In August 1999, the Education and Employment Secretary, David Blunkett, pledged to restore full employment. Whilst, as noted, there are

The new employment problem

HAMISH McRAE

We need more people. Without them how on earth are we going to fill the jobs and keep what is now the longest boom in British history going? ...

For the last generation, this country, along with most other advanced economies, has wrestled with the grinding problem of unemployment. As a result our minds are still beset by the idea that jobs are inherently scarce. This is reflected in the way job losses are reported – the 'New blow to Merseyside' headline – and the way in which much of the welfare system is structured. ...

Of course, there are still parts of the country where unemployment remains the gravest of problems, there are still one million people on the unemployment register; and there is a particular problem of the long-term unemployed. But these are specific difficulties that need specific remedies. Unemployment is no longer the general problem it has been for the most of the last two decades. ...

As a result the idea that there should be some inherent shortage of work, so that what there is has to be shared around (the policy of France) sounds very old-fashioned. The new problem, which I suggest will dominate the next two decades, will not be finding the jobs but finding the people to fill them.

Extracts from *The Independent*, 21 January 2000

still noticeable differences in unemployment rates between regions, it does appear a real possibility that UK unemployment could fall further. Indeed some economists argue that the problem which will face the UK economy in the coming years is, as the second quote at the start of the chapter states, not a shortage of jobs but a shortage of suitable workers. 'The new employment problem' expands on this possibility.

Policy on employment

The UK government has been looking to reduce unemployment by demand and supply-side policy measures. It has increased aggregate demand by raising government spending mainly on supply-side measures.

These measures include seeking to raise educational standards, increasing training, and encouraging people off benefits into work. To achieve the latter objective the government has introduced the **Welfare to Work initiative**. This involves offering a number of 'New Deals' to those in receipt of benefits. For example, the young unemployed have to undertake education or training, a subsidized job or work with a voluntary-sector organization or the government's environmental taskforce. The New Deals for lone parents and the disabled attempt to support these groups to take up employment by providing information, training and – in the first case – help with childcare and – in the second case – help with work placements. With these two groups the government is seeking to increase the workforce.

The workforce of the USA is currently growing mainly as a result of immigration. Much of this is illegal immigration, but the US authorities are turning a 'blind eye' as the resulting increase in the workforce has been keeping inflation down and contributing to the high economic growth rate which has been enjoyed.

The relationship between unemployment and inflation

Another aspect of the change in the recent performance of the industrial economies has been that the fall in unemployment they have experienced has not provoked a rise in the inflation rate. Lower unemployment has been associated with lower inflation than in the recent past. This suggests that the **Phillips curve** has shifted to the left.

The Phillips curve indicates an inverse relationship between unemployment and inflation. This curve is based on the statistical analysis of Bill Phillips who studied data on changes in money wages and unemployment in the UK for the period 1861 to 1957. Figure 27 shows the Phillips curve with inflation on the vertical axis (changes in money wages being taken as an indicator of inflation).

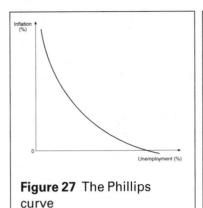

Figure 27 The Phillips curve

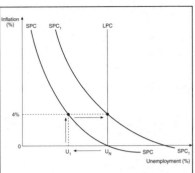

Figure 28 The expectations-augmented Phillips curve

The curve implies that a fall in unemployment would be accompanied by a rise in the inflation rate. A fall in unemployment would result in a rise in aggregate demand and increased pressure for wages to rise. Keynesians believe that a long-run trade-off exists between unemployment and inflation, so that a government could, by increasing aggregate demand, 'buy' a reduction in unemployment at the 'expense' of a rise in the inflation rate.

However, new classical economists argue that there is only a short-run trade-off. In the long run, expansionary fiscal or monetary policies will succeed only in raising the inflation rate. Figure 28 shows that an increase in aggregate demand does reduce unemployment in the short run but also creates inflation of four per cent. In the long run, as firms and workers realize that real profits and real wages have not risen, unemployment returns to the previous level as some workers withdraw from employment and some are laid off. However, expectations that inflation will continue at four per cent has been built into the system.

This idea that people base expectations of inflation on past inflation rates has led this combination of Phillips curves to be called the **expectations-augmented Phillips curve**. The long-run Phillips curve suggests there is no trade-off between unemployment and inflation.

The level of unemployment that is said to exist when actual and expected inflation rates are equal is called the 'natural rate of unemployment' or the 'Non-Accelerating Inflation Rate of unemployment' (**NAIRU**). This is the rate at which demand and supply of labour are equal and there is no upward pressure on wages and prices. It is shown on Figure 28 where the long-run, vertical Phillips curve cuts the horizontal axis, an unemployment rate of UN.

Some economists argue that changes in the structure of the labour market – such as increased flexibility and a reduction in the value of benefits relative to wages – have reduced the NAIRU rate. Others are arguing that recent events have actually called into question the concept of NAIRU. 'The demise of NAIRU' discusses the concept and questions its validity in the light of recent developments.

The demise of NAIRU?

LARRY ELLIOT

The concept known as the Non-Accelerating Inflation Rate of Unemployment was developed in Britain in the 1980s by Richard Layard, Steve Nickell and Richard Jackman.

Central to the idea of NAIRU was that demand alone would not cause unemployment, especially long-term unemployment, and that there were supply-side problems in the structure of wage bargaining, and the level of benefits that prevented the attainment of full employment. Any attempt to push unemployment below the NAIRU using macroeconomic policy would lead to higher inflation. The key was macroeconomic measures to deal with structural impediments to job creation.

This seemed to fit neatly with life as it was in the late 1980s, but in Britain and the US the theory has been discredited by events of the 1990s. The main problem is that it tends to move all over the place. When unemployment was around 10 per cent, the NAIRU was thought to be around 8 per cent; now that unemployment is around 4 per cent the NAIRU is thought to around 5–6 per cent. As unemployment has come down so have the estimates of NAIRU, which makes it useless in the conduct of monetary policy, even as an intermediate target.

In the US, Alan Greenspan has recognised this, and has stopped worrying where the NAIRU is or whether it exists at all. He has kept demand robust, constantly but gradually pushing unemployment down and taken a risk that inflation would not start to rise. So far, his approach has been vindicated.

The Guardian, 14 February 2000

KEY WORDS

Cost-push inflation	Deflation
Demand-pull inflation	Cyclical unemployment
Hyperinflation	Hysteresis
Quantity Theory	Welfare to Work initiative
Fisher equation	Phillips curve
Menu costs	Expectations-augmented
Shoe leather costs	Phillips curve

Further reading

Clark, A., and Layard, R., UK Unemployment, 3rd edn, Heinemann Educational, 1997.

Grant, S., and Vidler, C., Parts 2, Units 17 and 18 in *Economics in Context*, Heinemann Educational, 2000.

Russell, M., and Heathfield, D., *Inflation and Monetary Policy*, 3rd edn, Heinemann Educational, 1999.

Smith, D., Chapters 4 and 5 in *UK Current Economic Policy*, 2nd edn, Heinemann Educational, 1999.

Useful websites

Bank of England: www.bankofengland.co.uk/
European Central Bank: www.ecb.int/
World Economic Outlook database (IMF):
www.imf.org/external/pubs/ft/weo/

Essay topics

1. Discuss alternative government policies for reducing the rate of inflation in an economy. [20 marks]
   [OCR specimen paper, 2000]

2. In 1991 the UK rate of inflation was 5.9 per cent and unemployment was 8.8 per cent. By June 1998 both inflation (2.8 per cent) and unemployment (4.8 per cent) had fallen significantly.
   (a) Examine the costs associated with (i) inflation and (ii) unemployment. [50 marks]
   (b) To what extent are policies designed to reduce the rate of inflation also appropriate for reducing unemployment?

   [50 marks]

   [Edexcel, June 1999]

Data response question

This task is based on a question set by the OCR exam board in June 1998. Study Tables A and B and, using your knowledge of economics, answer all the questions that follow.

1. Inflation in the UK during the period 1985–95 was at its highest in 1990, and at its lowest in 1993. What evidence in Table A supports this statement? [2 marks]

Table A Index of UK retail prices (1985 = 100)

1986	103.4	1991	141.8
1987	107.7	1992	146.4
1988	113.0	1993	148.7
1989	121.8	1994	152.4
1990	133.3	1995	157.1

Table B Inflation in selected countries (percentage change in consumer prices from previous year)

	1975	*1984*	*1993*
Germany	5.9	2.4	4.1
Japan	11.8	2.2	1.3
UK	24.2	5.0	1.6
USA	9.1	4.3	3.0
Industrialized countries	11.2	4.7	2.7
World	12.2	10.6	13.0

2. An alternative way of measuring inflation is to consider how the pound loses real value over time. Thus, taking £1 in 1965 as the basis for comparison, this was worth 47.6p in 1975, 15.9p in 1985 and just 9.6p in 1995.

    (a) Explain how inflation and the real domestic value of a currency are related. [2 marks]

    (b) In which 10-year period between 1965 and 1995 did UK prices rise most rapidly? Explain your answer. [3 marks]

3. The UK government responded to the rising inflation of the late 1980s by taking drastic deflationary measures. The result was that total output in real terms, after several years of rapid growth, actually fell in 1991 and 1992, and did not reach its 1990 level again until 1994. How might an economist explain (i) the boom period of the late 1980s, and (ii) the downturn in the UK economy in the early 1990s? [5 marks]

4. (a) Use the information in Table B to compare the UK's inflation performance with that of other countries. [3 marks]

    (b) Discuss the possible consequences of this inflation performance for the UK's overseas trade position. [5 marks]

Chapter Seven

Fluctuations in economic activity

'These true believers argue that the information technology revolution goes not just wide but unfathomably deep – that thanks to IT, nothing humans do will ever be the same.' The Economist, 24 July 1999

Economic growth

Economic growth involves an increase in a country's or area's output over a period of time. It is, of course, possible for output to fall. In such a case 'negative economic growth' is said to have occurred.

The **economic growth rate** is the percentage change in output. So, for example, a growth rate of 2.7 per cent for France for 1999 means that France produced 2.7 per cent more goods and services in 1999 than in 1998.

Real and nominal GDP

As noted in Chapter 2, economic growth is usually measured in terms of changes in real gross domestic product (GDP). GDP is the output made in a country or area. **Real GDP** is the output measured at constant prices. This means that the value of GDP has been adjusted to take out the effects of inflation.

GDP is initially measured in terms of the prices operating in the year it is produced. This is referred to as **nominal** or **money GDP**. As some of the change in nominal GDP may be due to a change in the prices charged for the goods and services produced, economists eliminate this effect so as to gain a better picture of what is happening to output. This is achieved by multiplying nominal GDP by the price index in a base year divided by the price index in the current year. The box 'Converting nominal into real GDP' shows a worked example.

Ways of measuring real GDP

An economy's real GDP can be calculated by adding up total output, total expenditure or total income. All three *should* give the same answer because they are different ways of looking at the same thing: output generates income which is then spent on the output – this is known as the 'circular flow of income'.

Coverting nominal into real GDP

Year	GDP at current prices (£m)	Price index
1995	712 548	100.0
1997	803 889	106.3
1999	889 874	112.8

$$\text{Nominal GDP} \times \frac{\text{price index in base year}}{\text{price index in current year}} = \text{real GDP}$$

$$1995 = £712\,548m \times \frac{100}{100} = £712\,548m$$

$$1997 = £803\,889m \times \frac{100}{106.3} = £756\,246m$$

$$1999 = £889\,874m \times \frac{100}{112.8} = £788\,896m$$

Using the nominal figures would give the impression that output had increased by 25 per cent, but the real figures show it had grown by only 11 per cent.

Uses of real GDP data

Real GDP datas provide vital information for economists, business people, politicians and commentators. The information is used, for example, in forming government macroeconomic policy and firms' output and pricing strategies. It is used also to assess the performance of the economy or an area, and that is the use we concentrate on in this chapter.

Trend growth

Economists compare the actual rate of economic growth against its trend growth rate. **Trend growth** is the rate at which the economy's productive potential is expected to grow over time. In 1999 the UK government, believing that the country's productive capacity would grow more rapidly in the future, revised its predicted trend growth rate from 2.25 to 2.5 per cent. Table 19 shows the contributions to UK trend growth.

Table 19 Contributions to trend UK GDP growth (annual percentage)

	Labour productivity	Changes in employment rate	Population of working age	Trend growth
1990s	2.3	–0.3	0.3	2.3
Forecast	2.0	0.1	0.4	2.5

Source: Lloyds–TSB *Economic Bulletin*, December 1999

The two main supply-side reasons why labour productivity is expected to rise each year are (a) improvements in education and training and (b) advances in technology (see Chapter 3). Trend growth is sometimes also referred to as *sustainable economic growth* as it is economic growth which matches the rise in productive potential, and so does not generate inflationary pressures. However, we will see towards the end of this chapter that a wider interpretation of sustainable economic growth can be used.

Actual growth often fluctuates around the trend. This is because, at any one time, output can be above or below potential real GDP. If output is above potential real GDP because of excessive aggregate demand, the economy is said to be **overheating**. On the other hand, if there is a lack of aggregate demand output will be below potential real GDP, and an **output gap** would then be said to exist. From such a situation it is possible for the economy to grow at a more rapid rate than its trend growth rate. Some of the extra output it produces will be made using previously unemployed resources (closing the output gap), and some will be made using the rise in productive capacity. However, this high rate cannot be sustained in the long run. When an economy is using all its resources it can grow only at the rate allowed by its growth in productive capacity.

Comparative economic performance

Economists use real GDP figures also to compare the performance and living standards of their economy over time and with that of other countries and areas. Great care has to be taken in making these comparisons. Economists adjust for population differences by comparing real GDP *per head* (i.e. real GDP divided by population).

However, it is not so easy to eliminate the other factors which may give a misleading impression. For example, real GDP understates economic activity in most countries because of the existence of the **black economy**. This is also sometimes referred to as the 'informal

The black economy

Mark Macaskill

The black economy, estimated to be worth between £60 billion and £80 billion a year, has almost entirely eclipsed over-the-counter trading in some parts of Britain's most deprived areas. ...

Despite the government's attempt to clamp down on underground economic activity – and the appointment by Gordon Brown, the Chancellor, of Lord Grabiner QC to report on ways of limiting its size – the evidence is that the black economy is expanding rapidly.

An undercover investigation by the *Sunday Times* has revealed the vast network that supports it and exposed how whole communities exist beyond the taxman's reach. ...

Marooned on the M58 between Liverpool and Manchester, Skelmersdale, or 'Skem' as the town is known to locals, appears a joyless, grey place, little more than a cluster of barren council estates dotted around a ring road. Its residents, however, boast of its hidden advantages: 'I haven't paid full price for anything in years,' said Elsie, aged 60, who has lived on Skelmersdale's Digmoor estate for half her life. She spends every afternoon in the Duck, the local pub, drinking Guinness and smoking roll-ups. Her brother, who also lives on the estate, smokes more than 80 cigarettes a day but can afford it – he pays £25 for a carton of 200, a saving of 40 per cent on the retail price. ...

Cheap goods are not the only way to beat the taxman. Many locals cheat the system by claiming dole money while working for cash. ...

In the Duck, a barmaid admitted working part-time while claiming social security. She said she saw nothing wrong in that. ...

A report, *The Black Market in Tobacco Products*, by consultants DTZ Pieda, will be published this week by the Tobacco Manufacturers' Association. It will say that annual smuggling of tobacco, which costs the government £2.5 billion a year in lost revenue, is now second only to drug smuggling as a substantial criminal activity. Four-fifths of rolling tobacco and one-fifth of cigarettes smoked in Britain are illegally imported. ...

Areas where black market tobacco is most commonly sold have high unemployment and deprivation, a high proportion of lone parent households, poor general health and high crime.

Extracts from The *Sunday Times*, 30 April 2000

economy'. It covers all economic activity which is not officially declared to the tax authorities.

There are two principal reasons for not declaring activities. One is to avoid paying tax, and the other is because the activity is itself illegal. In the UK, the main industries thought to be involved are low-wage and low-income ones, often with a seasonal or irregular element to their work – for example house-building, hospitality, taxis and market traders. The black economy is thought to be very significant in certain parts of the UK as the extract 'The black economy' shows.

Another problem arises in comparing real GDP figures between countries and areas. A misleading impression may be gained if real GDPs are compared in a common currency by converting the real GDP figures using market exchange rates. This is because market exchange rates rarely reflect relative prices in different countries. For example, whilst the exchange rate may be £1 = 2.5 Swiss francs, £100 may buy more in the UK than $250 in Switzerland where prices are relatively higher.

To get around this problem economists usually compare real GDP figures using the idea of **purchasing power parities** (PPPs) . These are exchange rates based on the cost of a given basket of goods in the different countries. For example, if the basket costs £60 in the UK and 180 francs in Switzerland, the real GDP of Switzerland would be converted into pounds using the exchange rate £1 = 3 francs.

'Interpreting GDP figures' illustrates how the impression of the relative performance of a country can be distorted by the existence of a black economy and changes in exchange rates.

Real GDP and living standards

One of the main indicators of *living standards* is *real GDP per head*. However, the two are not synonymous. It is possible for real GDP to rise but for a country's inhabitants to feel worse-off because of, say:

Interpreting GDP figures

Although there is no doubt that the US, Japan and Germany are the world's three largest economies, the next three slots are fiercely fought over by France, Italy and the UK. The news that the UK has overtaken France in the league table of output, though, should be treated with a degree of scepticism.

Comparing the output of different countries is not an exact science. A reassessment of the size of Italy's black economy in 1987 meant that the country's gross domestic product overtook that of Britain, but its lead has proved a temporary phenomenon.

In the comparison of France and Britain, the exchange rate has been critical. French output has actually grown more quickly than British GDP over the past two years, the growth is set to outstrip the UK again this year. But the depreciation in the French franc (and latterly the euro) against sterling has more than offset this.

Financial Times, 15 March 2000

- a reduction in the quality of products produced
- a change in the type of products produced – consumer goods and services give more immediate satisfaction than capital goods
- a rise in pollution – negative externalities are not included in the measurement of GDP
- an increase in the inequality of income distribution
- a fall in working conditions
- a rise in working hours.

Similarly, one country may have a lower real GDP per head but its inhabitants may enjoy a higher quality of life. For example, US citizens have higher incomes than the citizens of Canada, but Canada regularly comes top of the Human Development Index (HDI). The HDI takes into account not only real GDP but also *life expectancy* and *education achievements*.

Causes of economic growth

The effects that economic growth has on living standards will depend on its rate, whether it is sustainable or not, and how it is achieved. In the short run the main general cause of economic growth is an increase in aggregate demand, as shown in Figure 29.

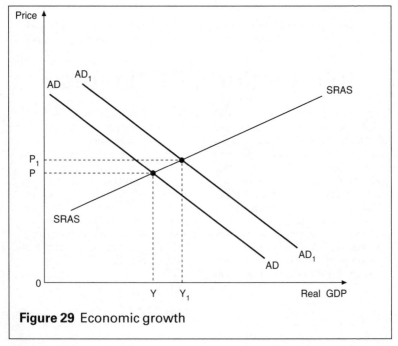

Figure 29 Economic growth

This increase in aggregate demand may be the result of a rise in any of the components of aggregate demand. An increase in consumption is likely to have the biggest immediate effect on living standards. Such an increase, though, may not be sustainable. The UK experienced a consumer boom at the end of the 1980s. Incomes rose rapidly, but the good times ended when the government, concerned about the rise in inflation, increased the rate of interest.

In the long run, economic growth can be achieved only if the long-run aggregate supply curve shifts to the right, as illustrated in Figure 30.

So key determinants of economic growth are thought to include *investment*, *technological progress*, and *education and training*.

Net investment (increases to the capital stock) raises both aggregate demand and aggregate supply, so it generates resources to meet the rise in demand.

Even investment which is undertaken just to replace obsolete capital goods may raise the productive potential of the economy. This is because the new capital goods may embody advanced technology which raises economic growth by improving methods of production,

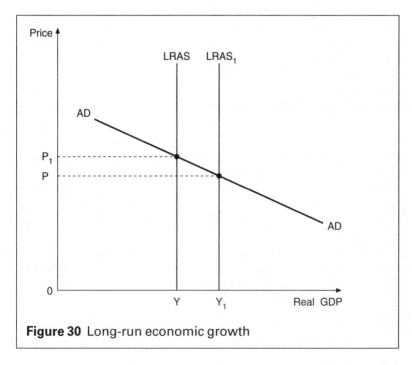

Figure 30 Long-run economic growth

Table 20 Economic growth rates in April 2000 (percentage annual change in real GDP)

France	3.2	China	8.1
Germany	2.3	Colombia	−1.1
UK	3.0	Egypt	6.0
USA	5.0	Mexico	5.2
Euro area	3.1	Singapore	7.1

Source: *The Economist*, 6 May 2000

increasing productivity, and hence reducing costs of production and creating new products.

Similarly, improvements in education and training raise productivity, and thereby improve the quantity and quality of products produced.

Rich and poor countries

Table 20 compares the recent economic growth performance of a number of countries.

As this table shows, economic growth rates vary considerably. Some relatively poor countries, such as China, may have high rates. Some of this represents an element of catching up. China is able to grow more rapidly, in part, because it has a surplus of workers employed in agriculture who can move into industry without affecting agricultural output, and because it can copy the ideas and technology developed in countries such as the USA, Germany and the UK.

In recent years China has become a more open economy. It has attracted a number of western firms to set up in its major cities and has increased its involvement in international trade. Other poor countries, however, including Colombia, have experienced negative growth rates.

It also has to be remembered that whilst China in April 2000 had a faster growth rate than the USA, its inhabitants still experienced a real GDP per head which was only one-tenth that of experienced by US citizens.

Indeed, over the last two centuries, the gap in incomes between rich industrial economies and poor developing economies has widened dramatically. The principal reasons for this are the barriers to economic growth which poor, developing countries face:

- *A lack of investment*. Poor countries by definition have low incomes. This means that their citizens cannot afford to save much. As a result

Table 21 Economic growth (annual percentage change in real GDP)

	1998	1999	2000*	2001*	2002–06*
France	3.4	2.7	3.8	3.4	2.6
Germany	1.9	1.4	3.2	3.0	2.6
Japan	−2.5	0.3	1.0	2.4	2.1
UK	2.2	2.1	2.8	2.5	2.9
USA	4.3	4.2	4.5	3.1	2.8
Euro area	2.8	2.2	3.4	3.3	2.7

* forecasts

Source: *National Institute Economic Review*, no. 172, April 2000

there is a shortage of funds available for investment.

- *High birth rates.* This diverts resources that could have been used to produce machines and factories towards providing schools and hospitals to cater for the rise in the number of children.
- *International debt.* A number of poor countries have borrowed heavily in the past from the richer countries. This has meant that some of the income of the countries has had to be used to pay off these debts. It has also led to a call for the rich countries and for organizations such as the World Bank to write off some of the money owed.

Recent performance of the developed economies

Table 21 shows that, with the exception of Japan, the western economies are expected to grow relatively rapidly in historical terms in the next few years.

The recent performance of the US economy has been particularly impressive and has led some economists to write about the development of a 'new economic paradigm' or **new economy**. This is the idea that the structure of economies has changed, enabling them to grow more rapidly without hitting a supply constraint and experiencing inflation.

The economists who support this view argue that the rise in economic growth rates experienced by principally the USA and UK reflect a rise in trend growth resulting from three main factors:

- *Improvements in information technology.* The development of the internet and other advances have made communication and production easier and cheaper and have raised productivity.

- *Increased global competition.* This has occurred again owing to the advances in information technology which make it possible for people to buy from sources throughout the world. The removal of barriers to international trade and capital movements has also increased competition in product markets and capital markets. In the latter case firms have increasingly been able to seek out the most cost-effective locations in which to produce.
- *A low-inflation environment.* A number of factors again are influencing this. These include the development of more flexible labour markets in the USA and UK, and lower expectations of inflation.

It is interesting to note that some developing countries, most noticeably India, are also taking advantage of the advances in information technology. In India considerable resources are being devoted to raising the educational attainment of secondary school children, particularly in terms of IT skills.

The extracts in 'The new economy' on the following page outline the empirical evidence for the existence of the new economy in the USA.

Business cycles

Business cycles refer to the tendency of economies to move from boom to recession, from above trend to below trend growth. This volatile nature of economic growth, which has particularly plagued the UK economy, itself discourages growth. This is because it creates uncertainty about the future and so discourages firms from undertaking investment and recruiting new workers.

Some supporters of the 'new economy' argue not only that the trend growth rates of the USA, UK and some other economies have risen, but also that business cycles have ended. This holds out the promise that recessions will no longer be experienced. The following are some arguments to support this view:

- Advances in information technology will continue to create new, more efficient methods of production and products.
- The demand for services, which are rising in importance, is usually more stable than demand for manufactured goods.
- Increasing integration of economies by virtue of globalization reduces countries' dependence on domestic demand and opens up new channels of supply. This reduces pressures on costs and wages. However, it also means, of course, that problems experienced in one part of the world can have a bigger impact on an individual country, as was witnessed during the East Asian crisis (see Chapter 5).

The new economy

GERARD BAKER

To the true believer it is a New paradigm, a modern industrial revolution that has lifted the US permanently on to a higher track of faster sustainable growth. ...

Since the beginning of 1996, the economy has grown steadily at a real annual rate of 4 per cent, up from an average of just under 3 per cent for most of the last 20 years. ...

The raw data seldom capture the full scale. Examined another way, the US in the last three years has increased its output by $1300bn, an amount equivalent to an economy the size of the UK. The sense of a unique American prosperity has been accentuated by years of sluggish growth in much of the rest of the world. ...

There have been periods of accelerated growth before, of course – for a few years in the 1980s, and for even longer in the mid-1960s. But what makes the current expansion unique is that this speeded up growth has occurred without inflation. ...

In the two previous long expansions of the last 40 years – the 1960s and 1980s – inflation gradually picked up speed, as the capacity of the economy failed to keep up with growing demand. Between 1960 and 1970, the broad, GDP-based measure of inflation, the price deflator, rose from an annual rate of increase of 1.4 per cent to a rate of 5.3 per cent. ...

In the 1980s, the price performance was better – inflation fell sharply during the 1981/82 recession and for a short while after. But by 1986 it was firmly back on a rising trend. Between that year and 1990, the rate rose from an annual pace of 2.2 per cent to a high of 3.9 per cent in 1990. ...

But the deflator has actually fallen every year throughout the current expansion – except one, 1993. Overall it has dropped from 3.9 per cent in 1990, to 1.2 per cent last year, and a new low of 0.8 per cent on an annualised basis in the third quarter of 1999. ...

For supporters of the New Paradigm case, this inflation performance, which suggests the rapid growth this time is sustainable, is a real change.

Extracts from *Financial Times*, 20 December 1999

Economists have earlier put forward the view that 'the business cycle is dead'. It will be interesting to see if this time the optimists are proved to be right.

The effects of economic growth

As noted in Chapter 2, economic growth can confer significant benefits, including higher living standards. One measurable effect has been the rise in life expectancy. For example, at the start of the twentieth century the life expectancy at birth for men in the UK was 51 years, and for women it was 58 years; these are now 78 and 82 years respectively. Not only are people living longer, but they are also enjoying better health in old age.

However, economic growth is not without its potential costs. Economists discuss the *opportunity cost* of economic growth. This refers to the consumer goods and services which have to be forgone in the short run to produce more capital goods to raise productive capacity if the economy is experiencing a shortage of resources.

Increasingly, though, attention is being devoted to the potential environmental and social costs of economic growth. If a country raises its output without regard to the effects that its production has on natural and non-renewable resources, and the pressures this may create, not only may its citizens suffer harmful effects such as pollution and stress but the growth itself may not be sustainable.

It is in this respect that a wider meaning can be given to **sustainable economic growth**. It can be taken to mean economic growth which can be continued over generations.

KEY WORDS

Economic growth rate	Black economy
Real GDP	Purchasing power parities
Nominal (money) GDP	New economy
Trend growth	Business cycles
Overheating	Sustainable economic growth
Output gap	

Further reading

Grant, S., *Economic Growth and Business Cycles*, Heinemann Educational, 1999.

Grant, S., Chapters 53 and 54 in *Stanlake's Introductory Economics*, 7th edn, Longman, 2000.

Grant, S., and Vidler, C., Part 2, Unit 16 in *Economics in Context*, Heinemann Educational, 2000.

Smith, D., Chapter 6 in *UK Current Economic Policy*, 2nd edn, Heinemann Educational, 1999.

Useful websites

The Economist: www.economist.com/
National Institute of Economic and Social Research: www.niesr.ac.uk/

Essay topics

1. (a) Explain the main factors that influence the rate of economic growth. [20 marks]

   (b) The economy of the Republic of Ireland is growing at a faster rate than the UK's. Does this necessarily mean that the citizens of the Republic of Ireland are better off than the citizens of the UK? [30 marks]

   [AQA specimen paper, 2000]

2. Discuss why growth rates may differ between particular economies. [20 marks]

   [OCR specimen paper, 2000]

Data response question

This task is based on part of the AQA awarding body's specimen paper for 2000. Study Figures A and B and the extract below from the *Financial Times*, before answering all the questions that follow.

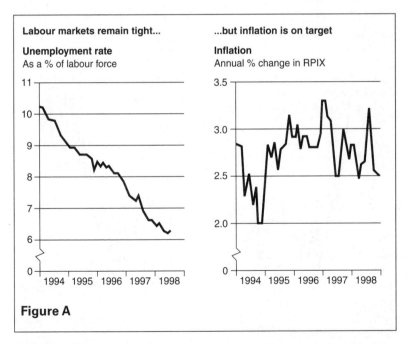

Figure A

What a difference a year makes. Last year there were fears that the economy was starting to grow too fast bringing about the prospect of an unacceptable increase in the rate of inflation. Twelve months later, and after two further interest rate increases by the Bank of England, the

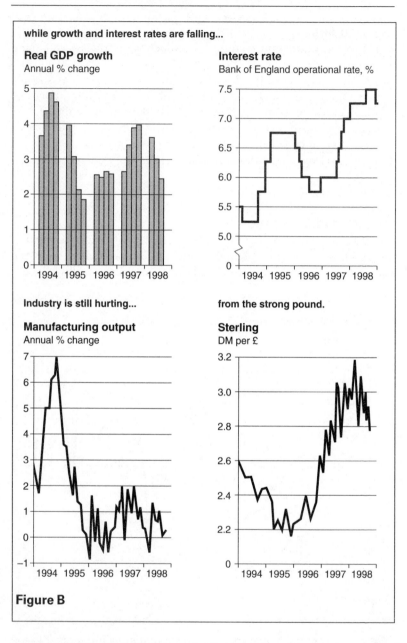

while growth and interest rates are falling...

Real GDP growth
Annual % change

Interest rate
Bank of England operational rate, %

Industry is still hurting...

from the strong pound.

Manufacturing output
Annual % change

Sterling
DM per £

Figure B

economy is slowing and interest rates are now being reduced.

Manufacturers have been most exposed to a tight monetary policy over the past 12 months. Interest rates have increased and sterling's exchange rate against the German deutschmark (DM) and other European currencies has risen by around 30 per cent. Export prices have become less competitive and the strong pound has also contributed to lower import prices. At the same time the UK's fastest growing export markets in recent years have shrunk as a result of the difficulties in east Asia. Some relief is now on the way as the Bank of England has started to cut interest rates.

The good news has been that inflation has stayed close to the government's target of 2.5 per cent. However, unemployment continues to fall and there are fears that wages, and hence inflation, may start to increase.

1. What is meant by the phrase 'a tight monetary policy'?   [5 marks]
2. Using the data and your knowledge of economics, explain how the UK's manufacturing industry might be affected by:
   (a) high interest rates   [5 marks]
   (b) a high exchange rate for the pound.   [5 marks]
3. Using the data, assess how well the UK economy performed between 1994 and 1998.   [20 marks]

Chapter Eight

Globalization and the national and international economies

'*The real problem today is that the system of governance inherited from the nation state is not up to coping with an age of greater economic internationalization.*' Larry Elliott, *The Guardian*, 6 December 1999

The integration of economies with the greater mobility of products and capital across national borders is opening up opportunities for consumers and firms, as discussed in Chapter 5, but is also placing increasing pressure on economies to be more competitive. It is also, as suggested by the above quote, affecting domestic economies, the role of domestic institutions, and the scope of international organizations.

Competitiveness
An economy is competitive if it is producing products that consumers want and at the price they are prepared to pay. The issue of **competitiveness** is very important for the UK economy. This is because, as noted in Chapter 1, the UK is a very open economy. Foreign firms compete to sell to UK consumers and UK firms compete in markets throughout the world.

There are a number of measures which indicate the competitiveness of an economy. In addition to the ones mentioned in Chapter 4 there are:

- the share of world trade
- the number of knowledge-based businesses per head
- consumer price competitiveness: an index of UK consumer prices divided by an index of competitors' consumer prices
- composite measures which take into account a range of indicators.

The two main composite measures are the 'league tables' produced by the Institute for Management Development and the World Economic Forum. The IMD publishes annually a competitiveness ranking of 47 nations (see 'US takes top spot in league table' and Table 22). The World Economic Forum concentrates on wealth generation as an indicator of competitiveness. As with the IMD's ranking, it makes use of statistical data and an opinion survey of international business people.

US takes top spot in league table

FRANCES WILLIAMS

The US remains by far the world's most competitive economy, according to the latest annual rankings by the Swiss-based International Institute for Management Development [see Table 22]. ...

The IMD, unlike the World Economic Forum that produces a rival competitiveness league table, gives some weight to quality of life indicators as well as economic performance. ...

Thus Prof. Garelli, director of the IMD, attributes the success of the Netherlands, followed to varying degrees by others in continental Europe, to a largely deregulated, open and flexible 'global' sector, accompanied by local services that preserve social cohesion. ...

The IMD defines overall competitiveness as the extent to which countries sustain the ability of companies to compete with foreign rivals at home and abroad. ...

The 47 nations are ranked using 290 criteria, two-thirds based on statistical data and the other third on responses to a survey of business executives. ...

Extracts from *Financial Times*, 19 April 2000

Table 22 IMD world competitiveness rankings, 2000

	2000	*1999*	*1998*
US	1	1	1
Singapore	2	2	2
Finland	3	3	5
Netherlands	4	5	4
Switzerland	5	6	7
Luxembourg	6	4	9
Ireland	7	11	11
Germany	8	9	14
Sweden	9	14	17
Iceland	10	17	19
Canada	11	10	10
Denmark	12	8	8
Australia	13	12	15
Hong Kong	14	7	3
UK	15	15	12
Norway	16	13	6
Japan	17	16	18
Austria	18	19	22
France	19	21	21
Belgium	20	22	23

The 2000 IMD report emphasized the role of investment in technological infrastructure. Stephane Garelli, project director, pointed out that the US and northern European countries dominate the top slots. The biggest climbers were Iceland, Sweden, Ireland and Finland. The Scandinavian countries are among the world's leaders in terms of internet connections, telecommunications and computer use. In their report, the IMD emphasized the positive impact the new economy is having on the competitiveness of economies.

These composite indicators receive a relatively high amount of publicity. However, some economists have questioned their usefulness and others have criticized them for attaching too much weight to free-market government policies (see 'League tables').

The following are some factors influencing a country's competitiveness:

- *Productivity*. Higher output per worker-hour reduces cost per unit and hence increases price competitiveness.
- *The quality of education and training*. A more educated workforce raises the quantity and quality of output and increases the mobility of labour.
- *Spending on research and development*. A high level of spending on research and development may increase invention and innovation, which reduce costs and create new, attractive products.

League tables

In truth these league tables (IMD and World Economic Forum) do little more than faithfully record the prejudices and whims of business leaders. Low taxes – Good, regulation – Bad. New Economy – Good, Old Economy – Bad. The frivolty in the annual reports arises from the pretence that these gut reactions can be turned into a single, objective number that has real economic meaning.

For one thing, nations do not compete like football teams, or even companies in the same markets. Economic growth is not a game with a single prize, or with clear winners and losers. On the contrary, all countries are likely to rise and fall together, even if the US is usually leading the way.

What's more, in themselves the rankings are almost wholly uninformative. For example, America is a fine country with a strong economy, but it has pockets of third-world poverty in its great cities and an education system so weak in parts that the US need to import, year after year, a large fraction of its most highly skilled workers from overseas.

The Independent, 19 April 2000

- *The inflation rate.* A relatively low inflation rate makes the economy's products more price competitive.
- *The exchange rate.* A fall in the exchange rate reduces the prices of the economy's products in terms of foreign currencies and raises the prices of its imports in terms of its own currency.
- *The level of net investment.* Net investment raises the economy's productive capacity. New capital goods also often incorporate new technology.

Measures to improve competitiveness

In recent decades UK governments have used a number of measures, mainly supply-side measures, to raise the UK's competitiveness.

- The government has removed official *barriers to competition* in the form of entry standards, minimum qualifications and product standards. The aim behind this *deregulation* is to increase the role of market forces and thereby raise efficiency.
- There has been official encouragement of *foreign direct investment*. It is thought that foreign MNCs bring in new ideas, new methods of production and new management skills, and thereby increase competitive pressure.
- *Taxes on businesses* have been reduced to encourage firms to expand and invest in new technology.
- *Flexibility of labour* has been promoted, such as through retraining and the encouragement of part-time and flexible hour working, so that companies can respond quickly to technological changes and changes in demand.
- The *quality of education* has been tackled by, for example, setting national targets and increasing government spending. A study published by the Organization for Economic Co-operation and Development (OECD) in May 2000 ranked the UK top for university education, but only twentieth out of 28 countries for secondary education.

The measures outlined above are designed to raise competitiveness largely by increasing productivity. There has been concern about the relatively low level of UK productivity. 'Raising productivity' discusses some of the measures the Labour government is taking in 2000.

Effects of globalization on domestic policy

In addition to putting pressure on governments to raise competitiveness, globalization is also placing a number of constraints on the independence of national government policy.

Raising productivity

MARK ATKINSON

If Britain's workforce can increase its productivity there will be long-term benefits for the economy. Improved education and training are the key. ...

Whichever way you measure it, Britain's productivity growth is poor by comparison with its major competitors and Mr Brown is determined to do everything in his power to close the gap. ...

Optimists believe the hi-tech boom means the UK is on the verge of a sharp acceleration of productivity growth, mirroring the success of the US. ...

But Mr Brown still believes the state has an important role to play, firstly by delivering a stable macro-economic climate, and secondly improving the economy's supply-side potential through reform of capital gains tax and encouraging entrepreneurship and extra investment in basic scientific research to ensure technological transfer from the laboratory to the marketplace.
...

The Chancellor's biggest potential contribution will probably be in the field of education and training. Mary O'Mahoney, research fellow at the National Institute of Economic and Social Research, who produced an exhaustive study of UK productivity last year, says the underlying cause of poor productivity performance is low skills.
...

No amount of investment in physical capital can make up for a poorly trained and educated workforce because without it new machinery is of questionable value. ...

Extracts from *The Guardian*, 14 April 2000

Fiscal policy

Globalization and the development of the internet have increased the mobility of shopping, financial and physical capital and, to a more limited extent, labour. This has reduced governments' ability to raise tax revenue.

For instance, if a country's government imposes higher taxes on firms, some of these are likely to relocate to the countries with lower taxes. High sales taxes will be likely to encourage consumers to shop abroad, high taxes on savings may persuade some to move their funds abroad, and high income tax rates may encourage a 'brain drain'. Internet shopping is making it more difficult to administer and monitor sales tax. This constraint and the competitive restraint are discussed in 'Caught in a global trap'.

A shrinking tax base will reduce the government's ability to finance its spending. This may prove to be a significant problem. It will become harder to reduce poverty and to meet the increasing demand for healthcare and education.

Caught in a global trap

There is ... growing resistance to paying taxes among richer people. Globalization and the spread of the internet will make that worse. Customers are already finding how easy it is to order products in one country through the world wide web for delivery in another to avoid local taxes. There is a strong movement in the US to make the internet a tax-free area to promote enterprise. And bookmakers and others are migrating to off-shore islands where they can pursue their activities out of the taxman's shadow.

Another source of income would be a tax on the hundreds of thousands of foreigners who are resident in the UK but whose domicile (real home) is abroad and who pay little or no income taxes here. This is a neat wheeze – especially if the revenues were hypothecated to sort out London's traffic problems. But again the Chancellor has to think global. Suppose that they all up sticks and move to the next tax haven. He knows that they are only here in the first place because of the ease with which people and capital can move from one country to another in a globalized era.

The Guardian, 25 February 2000

Regulations

Fear of discouraging foreign direct investment, and even encouraging existing MNCs to pull out of the country, is thought to be making some countries introduce regulations to protect workers and the environment. This problem is thought to apply particularly to developing countries.

Monetary policy

The increased mobility of financial capital has already reduced the ability of a national central bank, or the central bank of an area such as the euro area, to set an interest rate that is noticeably different from that of other economies. If, for example, the Bank of England raised its interest rate significantly above the rates operated by the American Federal Reserve Bank and the European Central Bank, it would attract a large capital inflow. Investors would seek to buy UK financial assets to obtain a higher return. This would increase demand for pounds which, in turn, would push up the exchange rate. A higher exchange rate would make UK products less price-competitive against foreign products.

The movement of large amounts of speculative money seeking to take advantage of interest rate movements and/or rises in exchange rates has also reduced the ability of governments to influence the value of their own currencies. In April 2000, Mervyn King, the Bank of England's deputy governor, ruled out government intervention to bring down the value of the pound. He said that 'the government lacked the firepower to take on foreign exchange markets'.

Financial institutions

The Bank of England

Globalization is increasing the importance of the Bank's roles in maintaining UK price stability and liaising with financial institutions throughout the world to promote world economic stability.

The Bank of England was founded in 1694 and nationalized in 1946. It has several functions:

- It issues notes and coins.
- It acts as banker to the government, such as by looking after tax revenue and making loans to the government.
- It acts as banker to the banking sector. All the main high street banks keep accounts at the Bank to make payments between each other.
- It manages the national debt – selling government securities and paying the interest rate on them.
- It determines the rate of interest, as discussed in Chapter 3.
- It implements monetary policy – including influencing the money supply through buying and selling government securities.
- It helps to supervise the banking sector. Together with the Securities and Investment Board the Bank checks that other banks follow sound and prudent policies, including keeping appropriate liquidity ratios.
- It manages the Exchange Equalization Account – which involves managing the country's reserves of gold and foreign currencies. It can use these to influence the value of the currency by buying and selling pounds when the government believes it is appropriate.

To maintain price stability the Bank of England seeks to keep rises in aggregate demand in line with increases in the country's productive capacity. Subject to maintaining price stability, the 1998 Bank of England Act requires the Bank 'to support the government's economic policies, including its objectives for growth and employment'. Bank of England agents visit firms throughout the UK finding out their views on, for example, future raw material costs and the effects of exchange rate movements. They also make suggestions about how firms can increase their flexibility.

Bank of England officials attend regular meetings with other central banks and the IMF (International Monetary Fund) to discuss economic developments, and hold special meetings in the event of actual or potential crises. For example, during the East Asian financial crisis of 1997–99, the Bank of England played an active part in advising the East Asian central banks on reforming their banking systems.

The Treasury

The Treasury formulates and carries out government policy and is managed directly by the Chancellor of the Exchequer. Probably its best-known activities are drawing up the budget and making forecasts. Among its other responsibilities are:

- controlling public expenditure
- financial management
- international finance
- civil service pay
- personnel management of the civil service.

Treasury officials meet with officials from foreign governments and institutions throughout the world including the EU, IMF and WTO (World Trade Organization). The Treasury has recently been involved in drawing up and implementing a number of initiatives to improve the performance of the economy. These include supply-side measures, which takes in the Welfare to Work policy, and the fiscal policy 'rules'. The latter refer to the government's decision that the state will borrow only to finance investment and not to finance current expenditure, and will keep public debt at a stable and prudent level. The intention is that these rules will promote economic stability which will in turn encourage investment.

G-7

G-7 is the group of seven leading industrial countries which meet four times a year to exchange information, to coordinate macroeconomic policies and to seek to avoid any disruptions to the smooth operation of the global economy. Its membership is Canada, France, Germany, Italy, Japan, the UK and the US, although occasionally other countries join the group for discussions. (It is known as the G-8 when joined by Russia).

The group has discussed and introduced policies throughout their economies to deal with a number of problems, including the overvaluation of the US dollar in the mid-1980s and the East Asian crisis.

The International Monetary Fund

The **IMF** was founded in 1944 and is based in Washington. Among its objectives are:

- to promote international monetary cooperation
- to establish a multilateral payments system
- to support smooth exchange rate arrangements among its member countries.

Despite its name the IMF is, in effect, an international bank. Members pay a subscription which entitles them to borrow amounts, in foreign currency, related to the size of their subscription. Small amounts can be borrowed without conditions, but the more a country wants to borrow the more conditions the IMF will impose. The IMF lends to countries with serious deficits on their balance of payments, and to countries seeking to raise their economic growth. In 1999, Russia was the IMF's largest borrower; in April 2000 it owed approximately $13.4 billion, which was about one-fifth of outstanding fund credit.

The IMF has been criticized for the conditions it imposes on borrowers. These have often involved requiring governments to implement deflationary measures. Such measures, it has been claimed, have actually hindered the borrowers' ability to develop by creating fluctuations in economic activity and cutting back on expenditure on education. For example, in the late 1990s, the Tanzanian government had to reduce state provision of education significantly as a consequence of its borrowing from the IMF.

In a world with increasing volumes of trade, greater interconnections between countries and the increasing possibility of balance of payments disequilibria arising, the importance of the IMF is likely to increase. Some economists argue that it should increasingly focus on helping to avoid financial crises and leave long-term development lending to the World Bank.

The World Bank

The original name of the **World Bank** was the International Bank for Reconstruction and Development. It, too, was founded in 1944 with the initial purpose of helping European countries to recover from the devastation of World War II. However, its main purpose now is to promote economic development in developing countries. It seeks to do this by giving loans for a variety of purposes, including land irrigation, education and telecommunications projects.

As with the IMF, the World Bank is rather inappropriately named. It is really a fund, taking money from rich countries and channelling it to poor countries. It is in the interest of rich countries for the poor countries to achieve increased economic development, since this will create markets for their products, will reduce the risk of negative demand and supply shocks, and will enable their economies to grow in a more balanced way.

The WTO

The **World Trade Organization** is becoming the world's international policeman – setting down rules and settling disputes between countries and trade blocs. Its predecessor was GATT (the General Agreement on Tariffs and Trade).

This started operations in 1947 and hosted a series of rounds of meetings designed to reduce restrictions on international trade. One of its founding principles was that a country must extend concessions it offers to one member to all others – this is the **most-favoured-nation status principle**.

The achievements of the rounds plotted against the growth of world trade is shown in Figure 31.

The **Uruguay round** held between 1986 and 1994 reduced tariffs and got the member countries to agree to prevent protection through subsidies or favourable treatment from government purchases. It also set up the WTO which formally came into existence in January 1995. In addition to seeking to reduce tariffs still further, the WTO was given the further objectives of:

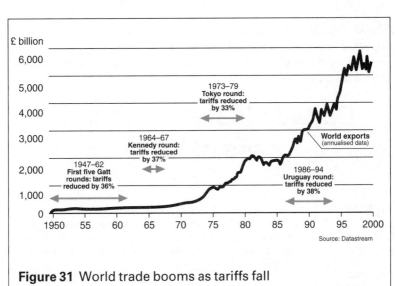

Figure 31 World trade booms as tariffs fall

Source: The *Sunday Times*, 28 November 1999

- formulating new rules in areas such as the environment, competition policy and trade in services
- operating a trade disputes procedure.

Member countries with a trade dispute have to submit it to the WTO and abide by its judgement – see 'Canada loses car import case at WTO' below.

The most recent world trade round talks hosted in Seattle in late 1999, and in Washington in April 2000, were disrupted by demonstrations. Those protesting were expressing some of the following concerns about globalization:

- The move to increasing trade liberalization may make it more difficult for countries to protect their citizens from products they regard as unsafe (for example, genetically modified foods).
- More pressure is put on developing countries than on developed countries to reduce their tariffs.
- Workers' rights are being undermined. If workers demand higher pay or better working conditions there is an increasing risk that firms will shift production overseas.
- Child labour is being exploited in developing countries.
- There is a widening income inequality between developed and developing economies.
- Harsh measures are imposed on countries that get into difficulties.

The WTO has the potential to grow into a very influential global regulator of world trade, but it needs to address the concerns that many have about the health, environmental and human-rights implications of globalization.

Canada loses car import case at WTO

Edward Alden

The World Trade Organization has ruled comprehensively against Canada in a complaint brought by Japan and the European Union over Canadian import duties on finished motor vehicles. The confidential interim decision, released to the parties this week, found against Canada on all but one of the issues raised by Japan and the EU, according to sources familiar with the decision.

Financial Times, 15 October 1999

```
┌─────────────────────────────────────────────────────────┐
│                        KEY WORDS                          │
│                                                           │
│  Competitiveness          World Trade Organization        │
│  G-7                      Most-favoured-nation status      │
│  IMF                         principle                    │
│  World Bank               Uruguay round                   │
└─────────────────────────────────────────────────────────┘
```

Further reading

Bamford, C. (ed.), Chapter 10 in *Economics for AS*, Cambridge University Press, 2000.

Grant, S., and Vidler, C., Part 2, Units 12 and 13 in *Economics in Context*, Heinemann Educational, 2000.

Nixson, F., Chapter 8 in *Development Economics*, 2nd edn, Heinemann Educational, 2000.

Smith, D., Chapter 7 in *UK Current Economic Policy*, 2nd edn, Heinemann Educational, 1999.

Useful websites

IMF: www.imf.org/
World Bank: www.worldbank.org/
World Trade Organization: www.wto.org/

Essay topics

1. (a) Examine the policies which could be adopted to increase the rate of economic growth in a country of your choice. [60 marks]
   (b) How might a sharp fall in world commodity prices affect economic growth in the world economy? [40 marks]
   [Edexcel, January 1999]
2. (a) Discuss what factors determine a country's international competitiveness. [10 marks]
   (b) Examine two government policies to increase a country's international competitiveness. [15 marks]

Data response question

Read the extracts below from 'Making globalization work for world's poor' by Larry Elliott, published in *The Guardian* on 26 June 2000, then answer all the questions that follow.

Until the debacle in Seattle last December, it was assumed that what was good for Bill Gates and Monsanto was good for everyone. Governments are no longer quite so confident that they are carrying their electorates with them and have been forced to reassess not just what globalization is, but how it can be shaped to maximize economic welfare.

Lots of the hardline, anti-globalization protesters are good at saying what they don't like, not so adept at what they envisage once capitalism has been smashed and the International Monetary Fund, the World Bank and the World Trade Organization have been reduced to rubble. What it would actually mean is that lives would be – as Hobbes put it – nasty, brutish and short. However, letting markets rip is equally daft. The story of the period 1850 to 1950 is of governments exploring ways of shaping and managing, directing and controlling markets to spread the benefits of growth and to ensure that the risks of economic failure did not all fall on the poorest and weakest.

Progressive taxation, welfare states, health and safety regulations, anti-trust laws and state ownership of key industries were all born out of the sense that wider democracy and ever-greater inequality of income were incompatible. With the gap between rich and poor today widening all the time, the challenges that faced reformers from Shaftesbury to Keynes now face policymakers.

How can a market system – which operates globally as well as nationally – be governed to maximize economic and social welfare? The task is much harder than a century ago because nation states exercised more control over their own markets than they now do over global ones.

That is one reason why the good side of internationalism – the spread of ideas, technology transfer, lower costs to consumers – has been accompanied by a dark side – money laundering, drug smuggling, trafficking in prostitution, financial instability. So unless some action is taken to shape globalization the world will become an even more dangerous and volatile place.

1. Define globalization. [4 marks]
2. Compare the roles of the World Bank and the World Trade Organization. [6 marks]
3. Explain two of the examples of global market failure mentioned in the extracts. [6 marks]
4. Discuss the implications of the increased difficulty nation states are experiencing in controlling their own markets. [6 marks]
5. Identify three benefits of globalization. [3 marks]

Conclusion

In this book we have sought to provide AS A level and other students with an up-to-date analysis of the various macroeconomic problems and issues facing the UK economy, domestically and in a global context. As the new millennium unfolds, this is a challenging time for economists. There are increasing signs that traditional economic relationships are being questioned more and more in a complex global environment. Nevertheless, we have sought to:

- review the recent economic performance of the UK economy
- provide a perspective of the economic theory and principles which underpin and seek to explain this performance
- show how various government economic policies are used and applied
- explain the importance of international trade and relationships with other economies for the current and future well-being of the UK economy
- discuss why competitiveness and globalization cannot be ignored in a present day study of the UK economy.

Each chapter concludes with suggestions for further reading and typical examination questions – some original ones written specially for the book by the authors, and the rest drawn from recent material produced by the main awarding bodies. We sincerely hope that the book will be of help and value in your study of Economics.

Index

RPIX 24, 38

Shoe leather costs 81
Short-run aggregate supply
   (SRAS) curve 7–8
Social Chapter 41
Specialization 53, 55–6
Supply-side policies 33, 40–1,
   111
Supply-side shocks 13
Sustainable economic growth
   78, 95, 104
Sustained economic growth 33

Tariffs 66
Technological advances 82, 99
Technological change 64
Time-lags 37
Trade balance 25
Trade creation 71

Trade diversion 71
Trade in services 27
Trade-off 19
Trading blocs 69–71
Transport costs 64
Treasury 115
Trend growth 94–5

Unemployment 19–21, 85–8,
   88-90
Unemployment trap 44
Unit labour costs 56–7
Uruguay round 117

Welfare to Work initiative 88
World Bank 116–17
World Economic Forum 110
World Trade Organization
   (WTO) 66, 115, 117–18